ELLEI
THE TRUTH

Stepping Stones to the Father Heart of God

Margaret Silvester

Sovereign World

Published by Sovereign World Ltd
PO Box 784
Ellel
Lancaster
LA1 9DA
United Kingdom

www.sovereignworld.com

Twitter: @sovereignworld

ISBN: 978 1 85240 623 3

Printed in the United Kingdom

Contents

Preface

Hunger for God

As a child I was sent to Sunday school, and thankfully I was given a certain amount of choice about where I attended. At the age of nine I decided it was time for a change. One Sunday, the teacher invited me to the front of the class with my friend. We assumed, wrongly, that we were being invited to sing a duet. But we were asked to stand back to back, and very firmly and deliberately, the teacher banged our heads together to teach us the lesson that we must not talk to one another while she was speaking.

The next Sunday school I tried was not much better, so I moved again after six months. I found a church then where I stayed until I was in my early teens. I remember hearing stories of Jesus from the Gospels, but I have no recollection of ever hearing the story of the love of God revealed in Jesus. So the God of my childhood experience was distant and impersonal. Yet during those formative years I had a deep hunger to know, in reality, the God I understood so little about. So much so, that I would spend long periods of time reading the Bible – in those days the only one available to me was the Authorized Version, which was not easy to understand.

Changed for ever

As a teenager I was invited to go on a Christian camp in Yorkshire which was to change my life for ever. It was there I heard the gospel for the first time and responded to it. I listened to the story of Abraham's willingness to offer his only son, Isaac, as a sacrifice. I wept profusely as I heard of the sacrifice of Jesus on the cross for me. At that moment the empty longing in my heart was satisfied at last. Two opposite truths impacted me – the depth of the love of God for me personally, and my own innate sinfulness. How could anyone know me as I really was and still love me? That is amazing love. I met Jesus that day, and I also had a revelation of the Father's intimate, personal love for me. I was overwhelmed as the wonder of such love filled my heart. From that moment until now I have lived in the security of knowing that I am dearly loved by my heavenly Father. This knowledge has given me an unshakeable sense of security and has kept me from sinking in the storms of life.

Grounded in the Word

The group of Christians who took me into their care showed me great kindness and practical love, for which I am grateful. They nurtured me and taught me the Word of God, for which I had a deep hunger. I was taken to many meetings where the Bible was unfolded as the Word of God, and yet there still seemed to be a missing dimension. I noticed that the Holy Spirit was never mentioned. When I asked about why that was, they told me that we had the Word of God and that was all we needed. One Sunday morning during the "Breaking of Bread," a young man who had been saved from a dysfunctional background prayed very movingly, expressing his deep love to the Lord Jesus. He was later taken to one side and told that expressions of love and emotion were not for public worship. This had a profound effect on me. The God who had saved me had touched me at the core of my being and I wanted something which seemed to be missing in my life.

A baptism of love

Even as a fairly young believer, troubled people seemed to cross my path. They could be fellow believers in the church, neighbors, colleagues or pupils in the school where I worked, as well as people I bumped into in daily living. People shared their hearts with me. I think I was a good listener, and I could point them to the truth of the Bible, but I had no answers that would enable people to be changed on the inside. I was busy serving the Lord in a variety of people-oriented ways and was outwardly successful. On the inside, however, I knew there was a missing link in the chain. When I was in my forties, the door opened for me to become a visitor in a prison for women and I had the joy of leading several of them to the Lord. Sadly I saw a number of them complete their sentence only to be readmitted, mostly on drug-related charges.

This brought me to the end of myself. I knew I couldn't go on unless God did something with me. I was desperate and set my heart to seek God. One morning I told Him that I would stay in the place where I used to pray until He met me. The Holy Spirit was poured upon me in a most powerful way and I was overwhelmed with love. Striving ceased and at last I knew what it was to be a channel through which God could work. The evening following this experience of being baptized (immersed) in the Holy Spirit I went into the prison, where I had the privilege of speaking to some fifty to sixty prisoners. The Holy Spirit fell on the gathering, and I knew this was a new beginning, a new dimension of ministry and service.

The anointing of the Holy Spirit

When my husband was called into full-time Christian ministry I knew God had a calling on my life, but at the time it was not clear. We both knew that we were in the will of God so, in obedience to His call, we moved to the place we believed He was sending us. Some weeks after this we were on a Christian conference at Lee Abbey when a delegate who was in full-time ministry shared some of his doubts and fears with me. He seemed to have lost his way and I felt a real compassion for him. Sadly, I had no meaningful answers for him but that night I had a dream. In my dream I was empowered by the Holy Spirit to pray for this same man. As I prayed he was transformed before me. When I woke up, I knew I had met with God. Although it was still night, I made my way to the small chapel in Lee Abbey. There God met me again in the same awesome way He had met me in my dream.

Calling to the healing ministry

Shortly after this experience, desperate, broken people were brought into the church where my husband was the pastor. I realized that my experience at Lee Abbey was God's anointing on my life for the healing ministry, and this was worked out for fourteen years in two local churches, before we were called very clearly to Ellel Ministries in the year 2000. I have been traveling this road of utter dependence upon God for twenty-six years, during which time I have witnessed many people healed, delivered and restored from deep brokenness. Many of them have had poor parenting at best, and some have never even known an earthly father. The revelation of the Father heart of God for them individually has been a major step on the road to wholeness.

I have lost count of the number of believers I've met over the years in many places, who had a desperate longing for their head knowledge of the Father's love to become a heart experience. The stories I tell are their stories. Some names and places have been changed to protect their identity, but every story relates to someone with whom I have had the privilege of sharing the Father's heart. I pray that *Stepping Stones to the Father Heart of God* will bring answers if this is also your heart cry.

Introduction

This book is written for longing hearts, for those who sometimes feel they cannot truly understand themselves or even make sense of life, and yet long to journey deeper into the Father heart of God. In it I hope to paint a picture; a true picture of what God is really like, a picture drawn from Scripture and as revealed in Jesus. We will look at some of the wounds which may have left a very different picture of God in our hearts. Although we are often unaware of these wounds, they come from our experiences of life, and how we have handled those experiences.

The chapters of this book will take you on a journey to knowing God as He really is. Having a heart relationship with your heavenly Father becomes possible when you overcome the blockages which are coming between you and Him. Each chapter is a stepping stone, taking you a step closer to knowing Him as your loving, tender Father. There are truths about your heavenly Father which you may know in your head but which you need to know in your heart if you are to live as His secure child. Each of us has beliefs which are rooted in the wounds of our heart. These untrue beliefs rob many of God's children of the intimate relationship He longs for them to have with Him.

When we are deprived of real childhood needs, this affects us deeply. Lack of nurture from our parents and lack of warm bonding with them wounds our human spirit. This can leave the soil of our heart prepared for a distorted view of God to take root; a God who is other than He really is and a God who, not surprisingly, many of us are reluctant to draw near to.

Unhealed wounds contain lies, and they are full of pain. Consequently we prefer to ignore them and get on with life. But unless we deal with the past it will always catch up with us. This book is a challenge to be real. Being real means owning life as it has been and facing our wounding, so that we can begin to experience the undeserved and unearned but unfailing love of God and learn to trust again.

Knowing our heavenly Father is not about our striving. It's about His unconditional love, His unconditional acceptance, and His unlimited forgiveness. When we know the true God, the real God, it brings an inner sense of being, which will open the door to intimacy in all our other relationships. God reveals Himself to us in order to transform us. He will meet us where we are. Throughout the book we will focus on aspects of God's unchanging character and His undying love. Through Jesus, we are not kept at a distance, but He wants to draw us to His Father heart where we can know and experience His love for ourselves.

I pray this book will be a revelation to you of the Father you have been looking for. No human father can ever compare with Him. You may have had a good father. You may have experienced a not-so-good father, or you may not have known a father at all. But God the Father is the perfect Father, and every child is precious and unique to Him. *You* are precious and unique to Him.

I pray that as you read this book, you will come into a new understanding of the heart of God for you personally.

CHAPTER

1

Father Image

It came as quite a surprise to me that people who have been believers for many years, who claim to know Jesus as their Savior, may not connect with the Father whom Jesus came to reveal. People who are blessed with many things – intelligence, charm, good looks, popularity and health – have a lurking feeling underneath the surface of their lives that something is wrong. Many people have a hunger which never seems to be satisfied, a hunger that has led them to look in the wrong places for love. The answer to that hunger and to the meaning of life lies in the Father love of God, because relationship with Him gives meaning to living. Wherever in the world I have taught the truths contained in this book, I have witnessed amazing lasting changes in many lives as God has revealed Himself to people as their true Father.

An angry father

Dorothy came to me for help. She was quite fearful, and as I listened to her heart, I felt prompted to ask her what she thought God was like. Her God was an angry God. One she was constantly trying to please, and yet conversely, one from whom she wanted to hide. There were many issues in Dorothy's life – sins she had committed, sins committed against her, and a number of traumatic experiences, which took her on a fairly long journey of forgiveness and into a new understanding of the true God – the God revealed in our Lord Jesus Christ. Dorothy's God had been dressed in her father's clothes. One day as we prayed she recalled a memory of her father standing in the doorway of one of the rooms in her childhood home with a cane in his hand, ready to beat one of her siblings. Dorothy ran into her hiding place and stayed there until his anger had abated. She had lived her childhood avoiding close contact with her father and hiding from him whenever possible. Like many of God's children, her view of God was distorted by her experience of her own father. She needed a new God – a God she could approach without fear. She needed the real God.

The father-shaped hole

In the heart of every person there is a father-shaped hole. Wherever you go in our world today, you will find the consequences of not knowing the love of a father. These are devastating; emotionally, spiritually and socially. Today, more than ever, people have a love hunger which never seems satisfied. Adults who experienced abandonment and rejection as children, particularly by fathers, are looking for someone who will be to them what their own father wasn't. They are looking for someone who will never change, will never leave them and who can always be trusted. Such searching results in repeated disappointment, for no earthly person can make up for the love that a person has missed in their developing years.

The Father of all fathers

When Paul knelt in prayer to the Father, for the Ephesians,

he affirmed that this is the Father *"from whom all fatherhood in heaven and on earth derives its name"* (Ephesians 3:14 -15 NIV text note reference). Every notion of fatherhood is derived from the fatherhood of God. God's father-hood is the source of earthly fatherhood.

God designed families, and placed fathers as heads of families for the good of children and of society. I have never yet met a person who has had good fathering and who has found difficulty in knowing God as Father. True fathers are those who portray something of the nature of God to their children. Knowing God deeply themselves and getting their own sustenance from Him, they are able to impart to their children what they themselves have experienced of their heavenly Father.

The following was written in a Christmas card by an eleven-year-old daughter whose physical, emotional and spiritual needs were being met by her dad in her formative years:

> *Precious Daddy,*
> *You are the best daddy imaginable. Thank you for encouraging me in my difficulties and supporting me in everything I do. Thank you for helping me to understand who God is, and for helping me in my journey with God. You have an uncountable number of qualities and I would never be able to show how much you mean to me in this card. Even though I often don't show you how much I think of you by my actions, deep down I know you are the best daddy in the entire world. You bring a smile to my face when I am sad and you have a special place in my heart.*
> *Lots of love from your little girl ...*

A twenty-two-year-old daughter wrote the following in the front of a book which she gave to hern father on her wedding day:

> *Dear Dad,*
> *A dad's work for a wedding often goes unnoticed. This is just a little "Thank you" for all that you've done for making today so special. It*

comes with a heartfelt "thank you" for your constant love and support over the past twenty-two years and for being a reflection of our heavenly Father's love and faithfulness.

Much love today and always ...

Earthly fathers are meant to be windows on the Father heart of God. Children loved, valued, encouraged and affirmed by their father will grow up to be secure and comfortable with themselves. They will form good, lasting relationships, and eventually be able to have a functional family of their own. Having prayed with numerous adults, I have discovered that many of them think the same of themselves as they believed their father thought of them. In consequence they reject themselves and struggle in human relationships, ending up with a broken heart.

The facts of life today

In society today fatherhood has been undervalued. A national newspaper commented in 2007 that many children are fatherless as a result of being born outside of the way God planned families to be. Single parents, absent fathers and broken homes through divorce leave deep scars upon children. Forty percent of fathers who don't live with their children never even mention they are fathers, and one in six fathers no longer live with their children. Eight percent of birth certificates don't give the father's name, and fifty percent of children are not born within marriage. And of those who are born within marriage, a number were not conceived within the marriage relationship.

Statistics from a leading criminologist showed that sixty percent of teenagers involved in crime and prison sentences have poor reading and low educational skills. Seventy percent are part of the drugs underworld through supply or usage. Eighty percent have grown up without a father and carry deep scars of failure and rejection.

Those of us who look at God through spectacles of childhood pain desperately need to come to a place of healing where the old image goes and a new picture of God replaces it. As we move along the stepping stones described in this book, we will journey from one image to another; from an image based on abandonment, neglect, rejection or abuse to an image based on the Word of God and revelation from the Holy Spirit.

That is how I love you

Joe was a young and gifted worship leader with a "father-hole" in his heart. During a course when I taught on the Father heart of God, he asked if he could sing a song which he had composed on the love in the Father's heart. As he sang, a much older man was unusually moved to tears as something of the love of God touched him for the first time. But Joe knew there was something missing in his own relationship with God. The truth he sang was not his heart experience. He always felt distant, as though there was something between him and God. Having come from a dysfunctional family with an emotionally absent father and a dominating mother, there was an ache in his heart to know God intimately and truly experience His presence. He decided to spend a day away from home, in prayer and fasting. After three hours or so, feeling frustrated and not at all close to God, he decided to give up. On arrival at home, he went up to the bedroom where his baby son was sleeping. He took his son into his arms.

As Joe looked at his sleeping son, spontaneous words of love came from his lips: "Danny, I love you. Whatever you may do to please me I can never love you more, and whatever you may do to hurt me I will never love you less. I love you so much that I would give my life for you." As soon as the words had left his lips, it was as though an audible voice spoke: "And, Joe, that is how I love you." At that moment Joe had a revelation of the personal, intimate, sacrificial love of Father God for him, and he was changed. As a father he loved his own son with unconditional love. Up to this time God's love for him was something that he felt he had to earn, and he had become worn out with trying to please God. He grew into a new understanding that God's love could never be earned or deserved. It is perfect love, freely given and inseparable from His grace.

Stepping Stone 1

Is there a "father-hole" in your heart? Ask the Holy Spirit to bring back to you some memories of your father. Give thanks for the good things, and make a choice to forgive the things that have been wounding to you. Ask the Holy Spirit to help you if forgiveness is hard.

CHAPTER 2

Grace is the Doorway to God's Love

In the cross we see God's love in action toward us, even though we do not deserve it. This special love is offered to us in the life and death of Jesus. Grace is another name for the character of God's undeserved love that is poured out so freely to His children. There are no requirements for being loved by God because it is a gift of grace that can never be earned or deserved.

Grace is an essential feature of God's love

I believe many of the people who struggle with the heart assurance of knowing God's love do so because they have a misunderstanding of the grace of God. Whatever we receive from God is a gift of His grace. We are saved by grace and not by anything we have done. Even the faith we exercise in the finished work of Jesus is not our own; it is a gift of grace.

> *For it is by grace you have been saved, through faith – and this is not from yourselves, it is the gift of God – not by works, so that no-one can boast.*
> (Ephesians 2:8–9)

Grace can be summed up as unfailing love and faithfulness. Grace is a miracle; grace is healing. It is the answer to many of our anxieties, insecurities, guilt and shame. It releases us from striving, from people-pleasing, perfectionism, and the tyranny of a driven life.

Grace saves us from the deception of performance and perfection

Evidence shows that the basic cause of many emotional and spiritual problems that trouble us as Christians is the failure to receive and live out of God's unconditional grace. Consequently, we fall into the performance trap and believe the lie that everything depends on how well we perform – so we are driven to do better and to do more. We are driven by continual feelings of guilt, condemnation or worthlessness, and we fear the disapproval of God. As a result, we go deeper into the deception of perfectionism.

In grace God lavishes His love upon His children

Grace is to do with relationship. Relationship with God is all of grace. It is 100 percent grace. Grace makes us God's very own children.

> *How great is the love the Father has lavished on us, that we should be called children of God! And that is what we are!*
>
> (1 John 3:1)

Our experience of God's grace affects how we see Him and how we see ourselves. When we have received conditional love from our parents, we are often left with feelings of fear, insecurity and self-doubt. We transfer this conditional love onto the One whose love is essentially unconditional.

William's story

When I met William he was dispirited, exhausted and about to give up. On the outside he was a successful and respected church pastor. He worked from morning to night and was constantly driven to do more and to do better for his church and for God. William had sought counseling on one or two occasions, and was left with the feeling that if he read his Bible and prayed more, then he would feel better. Sadly the advice given was not the answer to the problem.

William was a legalist, and this showed in his preaching. He was dependent on self-effort, activism and constantly striving to achieve. His problems were rooted in his relationship with his father whose love was always conditional. Unspoken words from childhood were still echoing in his heart as a man. "I will love you if …" "I will love you when …" "I will love you after …" "I will love you provided …" These conditions were acting as barriers to receiving the inexpressible love of God. William was living out of diseased childhood emotions.

The journey of recovery for William did not involve merely one step. There were many issues on the journey into God's heart. Firstly, he had to face self-reliance. He had to release his overwhelming desire to control, so he could change and become God-reliant. Grace had to permeate his heart. Obedience had to become an inside job and not just an external conformity. For William, a major step on his journey to knowing God as a loving Father was to be totally honest about himself before God, so that he could be totally honest about himself before others.

Truth of Scripture and life experience

For many professing Christians, the reality of Scripture and the reality of our life's experiences are not readily reconcilable. As a result we have a distorted view of God, a God dressed in other people's clothes. The clothes we dress God in are often those of parents or authority figures. We think God is like they were.

Deep wounds need deep healing, and father wounds are truly deep wounds. There is often broken trust embedded in these wounds, and many of us are left believing that our heavenly Father cannot be trusted. People experience a kind of spiritual sickness when they hold a wrong view of God. A wrong belief about God is a satanic deception and flies in the face of the revelation of God in the person of Jesus.

Your heavenly Father's love is unconditional, which means that it is unearned and undeserved. He longs to reveal His heart to you. Many people can see this truth for everyone else, but not for themselves. But God does not have favorites. Each of His children is unique and precious to Him. His love is immeasurable and He loves each of His children with the same measure of love. He loves you.

We are born with certain needs. Our two deepest needs are to be loved unconditionally and to be accepted unconditionally. For many of us, these prime needs have not been adequately met in human relationships. It is only God who can put into us what we have missed in human experience. The experience of His fatherly love and acceptance will be deep healing to our human heart.

God is love

And so we know and rely on the love God has for us. God is love.

(1 John 4:16)

God is not simply loving; He is love itself. His very nature is complete love. All His dealings with His children come from His heart of love, and He longs for each one of us to live in the deep security of knowing we are unconditionally loved.

Out of His bounty we read that

> *God has poured out his love into our hearts by the Holy Spirit, whom he has given us.*
>
> (Romans 5:5)

This doesn't mean our love for God, but His love for us. "Poured out" can also mean poured upon, a great flow, a large quantity, as on the Day of Pentecost when the Holy Spirit was poured upon all people. The love of God floods the hearts of His children and fills them, just like a flooded valley remains full of water. It is something He does for us, not something we do for Him. Of course we must be ready to receive His love. We do this by living in relationship with Him; by submitting to His will and living in uncompromising obedience to Him.

Suffering can make us doubt

Many of those I have sought to help have suffered in a way that is beyond human endurance, some from a very early age, and yet somehow they have survived by the grace of God. However, as a result of what they have suffered, many doubt God's love. The consequence is that their view of God and their understanding of His nature seem to be in opposition to how He really is.

The Bible doesn't avoid the question of suffering. It doesn't give us all the answers, but it does assure us that not even suffering can separate us from God's love.

> *For I am convinced that neither death nor life, neither angels nor demons, neither the present nor the future, nor any powers, neither height nor depth, nor anything else in all creation, will be able to separate us from the love of God that is in Christ Jesus our Lord.*
>
> (Romans 8:38–39)

In healing prayer, God often draws very near to the person who has been deeply wounded through what they have suffered. He reveals Himself to them so that they are drawn to His heart, assured of His love, and are able to receive his healing touch. We will look at the issue of suffering in more detail in chapter 10.

God's love is not the complete truth about God

In later chapters we will look more fully at the truth about the character of God, but there are three important aspects about his character which we must hold in tension if we are to experience feeling His love for ourselves.

1. God is light. *"God is light; in him there is no darkness at all"* (1 John 1:5). If we are to enter into a fuller knowledge of God, His light must shine into the dark recesses of our heart to illuminate what is there. Of course, this is a journey, but every journey has a beginning.

In Psalm 89:15 there is a promise: *"Blessed are those who have learned to acclaim you, who walk in the light of your presence, O* LORD." The holy light of God's presence illuminates the hidden corners of our heart, and exposes its dark secrets – those hidden things that we would like to conceal even from ourselves. Many have been held back in their walk with God and the revelation of His heart for them because they have been unwilling or unable to face the hidden things of darkness in their lives.

Jeff's story

Jeff was brought up in a poor area on the outskirts of a city, the youngest child in a large family. His mother had little time for him, and his father, a heavy drinker, was abusive. From a young age, Jeff spent a lot of time on the streets in gang culture or alone in his home. When I first met him, he was part of the drug scene with many problems, but he came to Christ and was radically changed. He had brought his life into the light and received much healing and deliverance. However, God seemed to be at a distance. Several times he came with the same problem – he knew he was saved, but the intimate knowledge of God as his Father eluded him.

There was something of darkness that he was not ready to bring into the light. He was afraid that if he confessed the deep thing of which he was utterly ashamed, I might be added to his list of people who had already rejected him. Jeff's trust had been broken on so many occasions in the past. As a child he had sought comfort in ungodly ways. When eventually the hidden things of darkness were brought into the light, he was broken in repentance before God. Jeff knew the forgiveness of God, but the final step before he was embraced by the Father's love was to forgive himself.

Later, as a father of small children, Jeff was able to impart to them something of the deep love he had received from his heavenly Father, rather than approach fatherhood from his own love deprivation. It is so important to bring things into the light.

2. God is truth. Truth stands constant and unchanging because it is grounded in God's constant and unchanging character. Truth can never be compromised. It is the same age to age, generation to generation and culture to culture.

Jesus said to the Jews who believed on Him, *"Then you will know the truth, and the truth will set you free"* (John 8:32). Truth about God can be known in the head and remain theoretical without having any effect on daily living. Truth needs to be experienced as well as believed. Truth is the opposite of lies. Many Christians are blocked from the reality of the truth about their heavenly Father, because they have believed lies about God – lies that are rooted in the wounds of the heart.

If God is truth, and I am to know Him, then I must live in truth and be truthful. The truth of who God is, when released in the human heart, is a force which sets us free from deception, falsehood, unreality, and bondage to sin and Satan.

When someone has been deeply wounded, especially in childhood, denial has often been used as a coping mechanism. Such a person may have little knowledge of their early years. They may even have periods of time blocked from their memory, and they will often say, "My childhood was very happy. Nothing bad happened to me." To come from denial to the truth can be a painful journey that a person must choose to make, in order to become real.

God can heal the real you, but He cannot heal something that is not real. Is there anything you say or pretend to God, others or even yourself which is not completely true?

3. God is holy. Holiness is the outshining of all that God is. It embraces every attribute of God. All His attributes come together and blend into holiness. Without being holy, God would not be God. God's being and His attributes function in holiness. Holiness makes God other than us, and yet He calls us to be holy.

The prime objective of healing must be holiness. Healing is wholeness, and wholeness should lead to holiness. There are no short cuts to this. Holiness in the life of a believer comes from knowing God through Jesus, and Jesus Himself addressed His Father and our Father as *"Holy Father"* (John 17:11). It is paradoxical that the One whose holiness is beyond our comprehension can be intimately known by us as Father.

Oswald Chambers wrote, "The call of God is like the call of the sea; no one hears it but the one who has the nature of the sea in him."[1] The call of God for all His children is that they should be holy as He is holy (1 Peter 1:15–16). All true children of God

---

1. Oswald Chambers, *My Utmost for His Highest* (Uhrichsville, OH: Barbour Publishing, 2006).

have God's nature within them. If you really want the nature of Jesus to be manifest in you, it will lead to holiness becoming reality in you.

Father is the most relational name for God

A true Christian could be described as someone who can call God "Father." Such a person has come into the family of God through faith in the finished work of Jesus Christ upon the cross, and God is truly *"father of all who believe"* (Romans 4:11). Other religions have names for their gods. Islam has ninety-nine so-called "Beautiful Names" for their god, but father is not one of them. Only the God revealed in Jesus can be known, and He can be known as Father. The analogy of Father and child is an especially meaningful analogy because it speaks of a most precious earthly relationship, and even non-Christians know how precious that relationship can be.

In earthly relationships, we know someone to the extent that they will let us know them, and they know us to the extent that we are willing to be known by them. Knowing and being known makes a relationship. God's final revelation of Himself is in Jesus who is *"the exact representation of his being"* (Hebrews 1:3). The longing in the heart of God is that His children should truly know Him and that they should live in obedience to Him. The Father and child relationship falls short if God's children are unwilling to live in obedience, with an open heart willing for conviction, correction and change by the Holy Spirit. But it is a relationship that is available for each one of us if we want it.

The desire to know God

The Bible and history are full of stories of men and women with hearts longing to know God as He really is, not to know an imaginary God. Moses is probably the greatest leader of all time. Out of his desire to know God more and to experience His presence in a deeper way, he makes two requests at a specific time in his life – a most difficult time.

Moses' first prayer is *"teach me your ways so I may know you"* (Exodus 33:13). The Hebrew word he uses for "know" is *yada* – to know intimately. Moses realizes that he cannot grow in close intimacy with God unless he knows the ways of God. To journey in the ways of God for Moses is to journey with the presence of God. God's ways are always in keeping with His character, and anyone who desires to truly know Him must be prepared to walk in His ways. God's ways and His thoughts are often very different to our ways (Isaiah 55:8).

Moses' second prayer was *"show me your glory"* (Exodus 33:18). He is yearning for a special revelation of God – a spiritual perception of who He is and what He will do for His people. Moses is told to hide in a rock and his prayer will be answered.

The Lord came down in a cloud and passed before Moses, revealing His Name and character to him –

> *The Lord, the Lord, the compassionate and gracious God, slow to anger, abounding in love and faithfulness, maintaining love to thousands, and forgiving wickedness, rebellion and sin ...*
>
> (Exodus 34:6–7)

This is how God was and is, for He can never change. It is how He has revealed Himself to be – compassionate and gracious, slow to anger. Even when He is angry, His anger is always righteous anger against sin and injustice.

He is more than loving: He is abounding in love.

He is more than faithful: He is abounding in faithfulness.

His forgiveness is limitless. However terrible the sin committed, His nature is always to forgive those who confess their sin and turn from it. This description of His character is given several times throughout the Old Testament, sometimes verbatim and sometimes in part. It is God's revelation of Himself to His covenant people of old, and it is how He desires His people to know Him in every generation.

Jesus reveals the Father to us

In the Old Testament, the word "Father," used in a relational way between God and His people, appears about fifteen times. In the New Testament, it appears around 150 times, because Jesus came to reveal the Father to us and died to bring us to the Father.

Many people say they do not have a problem with knowing Jesus, but knowing the Father of Jesus is different. But to say we know Jesus but do not know the Father is a contradiction, for Jesus is exactly like the Father. The two are one in essence and nature, one in character and purpose, though they are not the same person.

> *The Son radiates God's own glory and expresses the very character of God ...*
>
> (Hebrews 1:3 NLT).

Jesus is the way to the Father

In John 14 the disciples were troubled when Jesus told them that He must leave them and go back to the Father. They didn't want Him to leave, so in verse 6 Jesus is trying to help them in their time of fear. He tells them that He is the way to the Father. Jesus calls for faith to calm the troubled hearts of the disciples, a faith rooted in this revelation of the Father. This is a revelation that He has shared with them but which they have not been able to understand.

The revelation of the Father comes through Jesus. It is made possible through His total submission and obedience, made complete in His obedience to death on the cross.

Many years ago I heard the evangelist, the late Dr. Stephen Olford, give a powerful illustration about Jesus being the way to the Father. He was the child of pioneering missionary parents in Africa. In order to get to an unreached people group it was necessary to follow a guide on a path cut through a dense forest. After many hours of traveling, the guide was asked if he was sure of the way. On being asked the same question three times, the guide stopped and turned to face the missionaries. He told them to stop questioning him and to look at his scarred body. The deep scars were from wounds he received when all alone he had cut a path through the angry forest many months earlier. His words to the missionaries were, "I am the way."

Jesus says to you, "I am the way to the Father." He bears the scars of Calvary on His body. It is the death of Jesus that completes His revelation of the Father to us. His death was an act of infinite love and submission to the Father. No wonder John could say, *"This is how God showed his love among us: He sent his one and only Son into the world that we might live through him"* (1 John 4:9).

There is no fear in love

If you have a false image of God, you will spend your life struggling with fears and insecurities. The peace that Jesus promised as a gift to those who love Him will evade you. The Bible explains *"There is no fear in love. But perfect love drives out fear, because fear has to do with punishment"* (1 John 4:18). So we see that fear and love are incompatible. For some people, fear is linked to a feeling that there is something wrong with them and they deserved to be punished. But God's love has made provision for us to be saved and not to be punished for the wrong we have done. Jesus has been punished in our place.

In our earthly journey we will, of course, reap what we sow in terms of practical consequences when we make wrong choices. That sowing and reaping may bring suffering upon us. However, that does not alter God's view of you. Jesus has become the guilty one in your place and God's judgment for sin will not fall upon you as a believer in Jesus.

If your god leaves you fearful, you need a new God

Lena, a pastor's wife, was full of fear. There seemed very little else that could go wrong in her life. Her husband was hardly managing to survive in the church he led, as a faction group had sprung up that wanted him to leave. Their four children, young adults, were in different places of trouble, turmoil and broken relationships to the extent that Lena felt she had come to the end of her tether.

She was convinced that the current happenings in her life were a punishment from God for sins from her past. She was very willing to bring the things of the past that troubled her into the light, and receive God's forgiveness. She could not, however, move from the belief that she was being punished for her sin. Lena was sure she needed to be punished because she deserved punishment. She had been brought up in a home where fear and intimidation were powerful tools, and acceptance was based on performance. She had been saved in a legalistic church and knew little of grace.

Lena had a harsh, judging God whose love had to be earned. She was left with shame and guilt and a God to whom she could not come too close. Freedom from fear of punishment came to Lena when she had a revelation of the Father's heart for her. She saw the cross, with words written across it: "This is what I mean when I say I love you." She saw that Jesus was punished there instead of her. The God she had was an unjust God, who demanded payment twice for sin – from Jesus and from her. The wonderful truth of the grace of God set her heart free.

The revelation of grace opened the doorway to love, undeserved, unearned, unmerited and outpoured. The wonderful truth is that Jesus, in submission to His Father, was punished that we might be forgiven (Isaiah 53:5–6).

Stepping Stone 2

Do you need to pray for a new revelation of God, confessing that you have misjudged Him? Do you need to confess wrong beliefs, and ask God to renew your mind? Do you need to choose to believe that God is a loving Father, and choose to be His child?

CHAPTER

3

Fearfully and Wonderfully Made

As a child, my world was small. I was raised on a Manchester (UK) overspill estate. Apart from a very occasional day trip to Blackpool or Southport, we stayed put. As a young adult, my boundaries spread slightly but it wasn't until we visited our twelve-year-old son on a field trip in the Lake District that my eyes were opened to the wonder of God's creative power. Something in me was stirred. I fell in love with the mountains. I saw for the first time the wonder of creation, in which God remains personally involved. In my mind's eye a picture formed of this awesome God shaping the mountains, and creating the wind (Amos 4:13) and of the mountains singing together for joy (Psalm 98:8).

Many years later, my husband and I were walking along a mountain path in the French Alps when suddenly the path stopped. The Mont Blanc glacier glistened in the sun, and before us was an unexpected, amazing view of a tarn (lake) nestling in the mountains surrounded by brilliant colors. The picture was so beautiful I wept with joy. I was reminded again of God's mighty power, of His wondrous creativity and the limitless scope of His imagination.

However, on another occasion I walked for two miles one summer along the promenade near our home. Although the sun shone, the sea lapped on the shore and the Lake District hills stood out in the distance, at the end of my journey I realized that I hadn't even noticed the beauty around me. My shoe had rubbed a blister on my heel and all I could think of was the pain in my foot.

That is how it is when we suffer with inner pain. The wonder of who God is and of His creation is lost to us. We don't feel the joy of being fearfully and wonderfully made. We look inward and the pain seems to get worse, not better.

God created something out of nothing

> *In the beginning God created the heavens and the earth. Now the earth was formless and empty, darkness was over the surface of the deep, and the Spirit of God was hovering over the waters.*
>
> (Genesis 1:1–2)

We might ask ourselves three questions:

(i) Why did God create something out of nothing?
(ii) Why did God create human beings?
(iii) Why did God create me?

Everything God created was and is for His own glory – to bring glory to Him. That is the ultimate purpose He has for each person He has created.

He brought the universe into existence out of absolutely nothing. As we read the creation story in Genesis, we see the increasing complexity of what God created, ending with the creation of human beings.

God created humankind in His image

> *God saw that [what He had made] was good. Then God said, "Let us make man in our image, in our likeness ..." So God created man in his*

> *own image, in the image of God he created him; male and female he created them.*
>
> (Genesis 1:25b–27)

God planned in His heart to create human beings and He patterned them after Himself. When God said "in our image" He was placing Himself in a unique relationship with those He had created.

> *The LORD God formed the man from the dust of the ground and breathed into his nostrils the breath of life, and the man became a living being.*
>
> (Genesis 2:7)

God shaped man from the dust of the earth with His own hands and breathed into him the breath of life. Since the very beginning men and women have been dependent on God for life and breath and for all things. God made a clay model and breathed into it. How amazing! Life is a gift from God.

Humankind was the pinnacle of God's creation. God, who was perfect and needed nothing, chose to create someone like Himself to know Him, to be loved by Him and to love Him in return. Humanity, created in God's image, was not God.

Created for relationship

If God created men and women for relationship with Himself, that relationship must be the most important relationship we can have. True relationships grow. To be in relationship with God means to grow in God. Because God made the first man a human being, for that human being to grow involved having human relationships.

We who share in their humanity were also made for relationship.

In all of creation there was one thing that was not good –

human aloneness. *"It is not good for the man to be alone. I will make a helper suitable for him"* (Genesis 2:18). Adam had a perfect relationship with God, but without the woman as a companion and helper and partner in reproduction, the man could not fully realize his humanity. God then made another one like Adam to be alongside him as a helper and an equal.

In the beginning, life was perfect – how God designed it to be. Adam and Eve had an uninterrupted relationship with God, with each other, and they were at peace with themselves.

Created to share God's life

To share in God's life meant to obey God from choice. Free will was a love gift from God to humankind. Only those created in God's image could know God and share in His life. When Adam and Eve ate of the tree of the knowledge of good and evil (Genesis 2:9) their choice was deliberate. They made a free will decision, resulting in death rather than life for ever. The results of their disobedience have affected every single person since the Fall. The effect of their sin has not only separated their descendants from God, but has also brought pain and strife into all human relationships.

In the garden we see God's requirement for relationship with Himself – obedience. Our knowing of God is in proportion to our obedience to Him. It is not the obedience of a slave, but the obedience of a child who has learned to live in His presence and has learned that His ways are always best. We can also see the reality of what human disobedience leads to in the fragmentation of relationship with God and with others and the pain of separation that brings.

The choice of freedom

The one tree of which Adam and Eve could not eat was the tree of the knowledge of good and evil. God warned them that if they ate of that tree they would die. In giving the gift of free will, God gave us the freedom not to trust Him; the freedom to make a free will decision. Adam and Eve's decision, which was in rebellion to God, then became the doorway to the loss of freedom itself.

Crossing God-given limits always diminishes rather than enhances freedom. To stay within God's boundaries is to stay under His covering, within His protection. God's laws are laws of freedom and abundant life. They are laws of love and they work to the full when love of God is the motivation for obeying.

Good and evil

This phrase "the knowledge of good and evil" in the creation story probably means everything. It is the knowledge that only God has. They are words that point to moral choices, reminding us that moral boundaries are given for our good. They are God's pattern for living. When we overstep them we suffer as Adam and Eve did in the garden.

The serpent is crafty. He touches Eve at some point in her life where she is willing to hold back from God, where she is not ready to give everything to Him. That is how it often is in our lives. There is something we put before our relationship with God. He is our creator, our Father, and obedience is the basis of that relationship. The woman compromised something of great value – her relationship with God – for something of less value. Compromise is always on that basis. In the first instance it changed the course of human history, and in our lives too it will affect more than one individual. The issues involved in the conversation with Satan in the garden have been seen in every human being in both their relationship with God and their human relationships. They are the results of disobeying God.

Results of disobeying God (Genesis 3:1–13)

a. Doubt (v. 1) The serpent sowed seeds of doubt into the woman's mind and it was the beginning of the end. *"Did God really say, 'You must not eat from any tree in the garden'?"* Eve knew that God had said they were not to eat of the fruit of the tree of the knowledge of good and evil, but once she had listened to the serpent she added to God's word: *"and you must not touch it."* She doubted God, and it was the first step to a broken relationship with Him.

Firstly, Eve doubted God's character. The serpent does not deny the goodness of God; he simply sows seeds of mistrust. He tries to move the woman from her knowledge of God's goodness, and tempts her to doubt it because of God's restriction of freedom in the garden. It seems trivial that God should deny this small thing. The fruit of the tree looked good for eating. It was pleasing to look at and desirable.

When we go down that road of doubting God's character and unchanging nature, we have gone too far. God has set limits, and to live under God's blessing is to live in obedience to Him.

Secondly, Eve doubted God's word. It seemed unreasonable that God should forbid them tasting the fruit. By this time, her trust in God had diminished. Doubt led to disobedience.

Doubt can be a major enemy to obedience in our lives. It is one of Satan's tactics to draw us away from God. If we doubt God, we will find it very hard to trust Him and take steps of obedience. It is not possible to have an intimate relationship with God without trust. This is also true in human relationships. Many people find it extremely difficult to trust God or people. This is usually because as a child their trust has been shattered or because their childhood environment has not been safe enough for them to develop the capacity to trust. Basic mistrust at the core of our being becomes a root from which emotional, relational and spiritual problems will develop throughout life. We will look at this in more depth in chapter 8.

b. Pride (v. 5) *"For God knows that when you eat of [the fruit] your eyes will be opened, and you will be like God, knowing good and evil."*

"God knows!" Satan accuses God of having unworthy motives. Their eyes were opened, that was true, but in quite a different way to what the serpent promised. Only God is omniscient. Humans can never be the same as God. They must remain dependent upon Him.

Pride has always been the number one enemy of the human heart. God hates pride. It has many facets and is sometimes difficult to recognize until the Holy Spirit brings conviction. Pride is destructive because it has great power to damage our relationships with God and with other people. It separates us from God and separates us from others. C.S. Lewis pointed out that if anyone thinks they are not proud, they are very proud indeed.

c. Shame (v. 7) *"The eyes of both of them were opened, and they realized they were naked; so they sewed fig leaves together and made coverings for themselves."*

They lost their innocence. They had a new awareness of themselves and of each other in their nakedness and shame. They sewed fig leaves together. It was their own feeble effort to hide their shame. Only God could cover their shame, and He made garments of skin to cover them (v. 21).

Shame is a sense of not being comfortable with yourself at the core of your being. Because you are not comfortable with yourself as you are, you are not comfortable in the company of others.

Many of us feel worthless and hopeless. We cannot accept the affirming words, "I am fearfully and wonderfully made." We dislike ourselves and cannot imagine we are acceptable to others. Because we are not comfortable with being ourselves, we hide.

Shame is still the fruit of lost innocence. Loss of innocence produces a shame-based identity. This gives the message, "I am wrong; I am a mistake." When that happens, we don't only feel separated from God and others, we feel separated from ourselves.

d. Fear (v. 10) *"I was afraid because I was naked ..."*

Even though Adam and Eve were made in the image of God for unbroken relationship with Him, they now feared Him. When they heard the sound of the Lord God walking in the garden, instead of being ready to welcome Him, they hid from Him in fear. When they ate of the forbidden fruit, they separated themselves from God through disobedience. They feared because all their security had gone. There was now a separation between them and God.

Deep fear in the human heart often comes from separation. Many people we minister to cannot remember a time when they were not fearful. At critical times in their lives they may have been physically separated from parents and family, leaving them with the sense of abandonment. Those who have lacked emotional parental bonding have a fear that constantly lurks in the heart. Others live with pre-natal fear, fear that was picked up in their mother's womb. Such fear is often seen in one generation after another. Fear limits life. It robs a person of the fullness Jesus spoke of in John 10:10: *"I have come that they may have life, and have it to the full."*

Cindy's story

Cindy, a mother of three, was active in Christian work alongside her husband. She managed to cover her fear fairly well, but she could not remember a time in her life when she was not fearful. Over the years, she had received prayer and yet the problem remained. When I met Cindy, she had acute physical symptoms and was convinced she could have a serious illness and might die. The fear was overwhelming. As we prayed with Cindy, she was taken back to the time in her mother's womb where she had picked up her mother's fear, and to the first few weeks after she was born when her depressed mother had been unable to bond with her.

Throughout the years fear had become a stronghold over Cindy's mind, which was full of imaginary thoughts and unreal things. A stronghold is a mindset filled with hopelessness that causes us to accept as unchangeable something which is against the will of God (see 2 Corinthians 10:5–6). The enemy will be hiding behind a stronghold, and his purpose is to keep us from the true knowledge of God.

As we ministered, God revealed Himself to Cindy as the loving Father who will always protect. As Father God revealed Himself to her, the stronghold was broken, she was released from fear in a wonderful way, and the physical symptoms disappeared completely.

Cindy recognized that the symptoms of fear which had been in her life were also in one of her children. Her four-year-old daughter needed Cindy to stay with her each evening until she went to sleep. The child regularly woke up fearful during the night. One night while her little girl was sleeping, Cindy and her husband prayed for the child in the way she herself had been prayed for. From that time on the child's fear was banished, never to return.

e. Guilt (v. 10) *"I heard you in the garden ... so I hid."*

They were guilty of an estranged relationship with God.

Adam and Eve heard the sound of their creator walking in the garden. The sound of the Lord God walking in the garden seeking their fellowship was no longer received with joy. The garden, once a place of joy and fellowship with God, became a place of fear and hiding from Him. It was a threat. Knowing they were guilty, they hid. It was a foolish action of course, because no one can hide from God.

To hide from God is guilt's response to Him. Guilt separates us from Him but we need not hide, for the way has been made open for us to draw near without fear, and receive forgiveness and reconciliation.

f. Blame (vv. 12–13) The man said, "'*The woman you put here with me – she gave me some fruit from the tree, and I ate it ... The woman said, 'The serpent deceived me, and I ate.'*"

They evaded their responsibility by blame shifting. The man blames God and the woman (anyone but himself) for his sin. The woman blames the serpent rather than herself.

That is how it has been since Adam and Eve ate of the fruit that would make them wise. Blame shifting gets us nowhere. As we take responsibility for our own moral actions, we find forgiveness and redemption in the God who created us. Do we ever blame others?

Blaming God

People who have suffered at the hands of others will often blame God for their suffering. They have a picture of a helpless or vengeful God who looks on their suffering and does nothing about it.

The truth is that our heavenly Father hates injustice, and He suffers with us when we suffer. As we have seen, freedom of choice was a gift to humankind at creation. Therefore, everyone is free to make his or her own choices, even if this is at the expense of someone else. God will not override anyone's free will. Consequently, bad things happen to good/innocent people.

Some years ago I was in the park with six of our grandchildren. The eldest, who was nine at the time, was pushing the roundabout as the younger children shrieked with delight. As I tried to slow down the roundabout, I warned Sarah Jane more than once that it was going too fast and she could get hurt. The inevitable happened. The younger children saw it as part of the game and laughed. Her pride was hurt and she stormed away to nurse her wounds. Sarah Jane was convinced I was to blame for the accident. "It's your fault, Granny. You could have stopped it." I asked her if she thought I loved her. As I loved her so much I asked did she think I would ever hurt her. We were immediately reconciled and the incident was not mentioned again.

The truth is that some of us treat God that way. We blame him for things that are often the result of our disobedience to Him, or our own wrong choices. We are all responsible for our choices. However, we are who we are to some degree because of who our parents were and what we have learned of life, of love and of God from them. Like Cindy, we can be trapped in the same emotional bondage as they were.

Sometimes sin traps us so that we are not open to that which is good. The iniquity of our fathers is sometimes visited upon us as children. We then become trapped in patterns of behavior, emotional responses or physical maladies that affect the quality of our lives.

The results of the sin of Adam and Eve in the garden have affected all of our lives. The wonder is that God did something about our condition. *"For as in Adam all die, so in Christ all will be made alive"* (1 Corinthians 15:22).

Through Jesus we are brought near to God. Through Jesus life can begin again for all of us. Through Jesus we can know our creator who made us fearfully and wonderfully in His image. Through Jesus we can know Him as our Father.

Stepping Stone 3

Thank God that you are made in His image for relationship with Him. Ask Him to show you anything in your life that puts a distance between you and the experience of His unchanging love for you.

CHAPTER

4

Created Needy by Design

God in His wisdom created Adam with needs, and that neediness has passed to all Adam's descendants. We have seen how God created him with a need for human relationship to fill his loneliness. In other words, God created Adam with emotional needs. Adam was created with physical needs and God met those with food from the garden. He was also created with a spiritual need and God met that need as He fellowshipped with Adam and Eve in the garden before sin entered.

God is all I need

I have met several people who have strongly asserted that God is all they need. They often say they enjoy being alone. These have usually been people who are not too good with relationships. Certainly our relationship with God is primary. For all of us, our deepest need is to know Him intimately and be one with Him. He is the ultimate source for meeting all our needs. However, to deny our humanity and the fact that we have human needs may sound super-spiritual, but it is also unreal. God could have made us differently, but He chose it the way it is.

Families were God's design. God intended our human needs to be met at first within these family structures. When our needs are adequately met in childhood, a solid foundation is laid upon which life can be built.

God designed relationships to be intimate. The Father image of God is the one we can mostly identify with because it is a human image. It is intimacy in our relationship with God that touches our heart. From this relationship other relationships grow. Intimacy makes relationships real and close. Some of us find it hard to have real and close relationships because our relational needs have been left unmet. Our emotional need, our need for emotional intimacy, has not been met.

Emotional needs are also called developmental needs. They are foundational building blocks that make us what we are. Unmet needs in our early years cause emotional wounds and have a lingering impact on our lives.

Three foundational building blocks

Most parents try to do the best for their children. Many parents, however, approach parenthood out of their own deprivation and do not have the emotional tools with which to lay the right foundation in the lives of their children. Some of their own emotional needs have often been unmet, and so they function out of their own negative emotions, often struggling to understand themselves.

There are three foundational building blocks: the need for unconditional love, the need for self-worth and the need for security.

1. THE NEED FOR UNCONDITIONAL LOVE

This foundational need is met through

a. Acceptance: We each have a deep relational need for others to accept us for who we are and what we are. Acceptance, therefore, must be unconditional. At best many people experience conditional acceptance. Others experience outright rejection. Acceptance of a person is to receive the other as of great worth and value for who they are, and not for what they do or give.

b. Approval: Approval is to think and speak well of someone. To approve a person is to convey positive attitudes to the person through words, looks, attitudes and actions. We are born with a need for others to express their love with words and actions that communicate, "I am pleased with you."

Someone has said that it takes fifteen words of approval to counteract one word of disapproval.

c. Provision: Provision is not simply meeting physical needs, but also emotional and spiritual needs. Providing for the needs of body, soul and spirit.

2. THE NEED FOR SELF-WORTH

This foundational need is met through

a. Attention: To give someone attention is to give undivided attention. It is to focus on that person and their concerns. It is also to share their interests and to enter into their world. Children who receive attention in their early years do not grow up demanding attention inappropriately.

b. Encouragement: To encourage is inspirational. It is to assure a person that they have the ability to succeed in that which they are gifted for. Parents who have expected perfection from their children have sowed foundational seeds of frustration and failure that can lead to pain and disappointment in adult life.

c. Affirmation: To affirm is to speak well of, to affirm a person in their identity and gifting and to positively urge forward.

3. THE NEED FOR SECURITY
This foundational need is met through

a. Comfort: The need for comfort is the first felt need a baby has when it comes into the world. A crying child is comforted when he or she is held close, when gentle words are spoken and when his or her physical needs are met. Over time, a child stores memories of being comforted.

b. Bonding: Bonding is the ability to establish an emotional attachment to another person – to relate at a deep level. On entering the world, a baby needs a safe place in the lives of others where it can be in relationship.

Attachment is another word for bonding. At the beginning of life, parents should welcome their children into the world. That welcome conveys a message to the spirit of the child, "You belong to us, you are part of us, you are safe with us." Bonding takes place as developmental needs are met.

If we do not experience bonding as infants, we go through life with feelings of deep insecurity, separation and anxiety.

c. Nurture: Nurture is goodness and sustenance. Nothing in the universe grows without a source of strength and nutrition. For a plant to grow, it must draw from something outside of itself – it needs water, sunshine and nutrients. It needs to be planted in good soil if it is to flourish. These things feed the plant and give it strength. We also need a source of nourishment and strength in childhood; physically, emotionally and spiritually. We need nurture.

Nurtured by a mother and father in the first few months of life, a child receives a sense of security, safety, peace and contentment, and is blessed. Conversely, lack of nurture in infancy cripples us emotionally and affects the whole developmental process.

Needs, met and unmet, in our early years greatly impact our thinking, feeling and behavior as we grow from childhood to adult life. When needs are met, we feel good. We have a sense of being loved and cared for and feel content with being who God made us to be. When they are not met, we feel bad and we develop a sense of frustration, discontent, fear and dissatisfaction. There is potential and pain in intimacy needs.

The potential of needs met

If our childhood needs are met in a godly way, we develop healthy thinking about ourselves. We feel important and grow in confidence that we can and will do well, because we have experienced unconditional love.

This in turn leads to positive emotions, emotions of feeling worthy, confident and secure. What we think and feel leads to productive behavior that blesses and reaches out to other people. The outcomes of our needs being met are positive. We are able to build a functional family, we have a good self-image and build intimate relationships. These strengths become foundational for the next generation.

The pain of unmet needs

If we have suffered neglect, abuse, rejection, absence, criticism and other negative behavior, our thinking becomes unhealthy. Thoughts like these spring to mind: "What's wrong with me?" "I don't matter;" "I'll try harder and perhaps then I'll be loved."

We become what we think. Unhealthy thinking leads to troubled emotions. Such thoughts and beliefs result in feelings of being unworthy, anxious, condemned and fearful. It all leaves us feeling vulnerable and unloved. Because of the deep inner pain, we develop unproductive behavior patterns.

These include control and manipulation of others, addictions, compulsions and self-abuse. The painful outcome of unmet needs is seen in a poor self-image, personality disturbances, and problems with daily living which inevitably lead to a dysfunctional family for the next generation.

If some of our infancy and childhood needs remain unmet, we enter adulthood lacking some of the resources we need to become mature. We cannot give away what we have not received. Unmet needs and emotional wounds from our early years have a lingering impact upon our lives.

Through Jesus we are restored

God has made a way for us to be restored. No earthly person can give us what we have missed in childhood. However, our need for unconditional love, self-worth and security are all met in Jesus.

When the Father gave His Son to die for you on the cross, He showed love that you could never earn or deserve – unconditional love. He accepts you unconditionally, approves of you and provides for you. And for me. That, of course, is the beginning of our new life. The quality of our relationship with God, being able to experience His love day by day, is conditional. We do have our part to play. We have to turn to Him.

The death of Jesus on the cross validates that you have unimaginably great worth. In relationship with Jesus, you are assured of worthiness. Jesus reconciled you to God, and therefore God holds nothing against you at all. All the affirmation He made you to need is to be found in Him.

However deep-seated our insecurity, true security is to be found in relationship with our heavenly Father. We may have known little of comfort, bonding and nurture in our formative years. The results may be really devastating. But as we turn toward the Father Jesus revealed, we gain more heart knowledge of how dearly He has loved us. That helps us to let go of the false things we have looked to for security, and life takes on new meaning.

Joyce's story

I met Joyce immediately after she had become a Christian. Her conversion was quite miraculous – a direct intervention of God in a human life. Her childhood had been horrific. She had witnessed and heard things at the hand of her father that no child should ever see or hear. Eventually her mother went into hiding and took the children with her. Joyce was overwhelmed with anxiety and insecurity. As the eldest child she took on the role of caring for the family, including her mother, who was quite inadequate.

In Joyce's heart there was a love hunger which became a love addiction and took her into many ungodly relationships. Coupled with this lifestyle, she had become deeply involved in the occult, which gave her some control over other people.

Immediately after she was born again, Joyce repented of her lifestyle and was set free from many of the ungodly things she had been involved with. She had no role model of a father whatsoever, but her desire was to know God increasingly. She was committed to dealing with anything in her life that displeased Him. The revelation of His love to her as His child was overwhelming, freeing her from deep fears and insecurities.

Father God deeply cares

Father God knows each of us individually and intimately. He longs to father us again and bring restoration into our wounded hearts. Our heavenly Father understands our need, and enfolded in His love we hear the answer to our heart's cry. As we seek Him day by day, He will continue to nurture us and to provide the love and guidance, the correction and instruction we need to grow into maturity in Him.

With a small team I had the privilege of ministering for a few days in a church in Romania. Many of the people had suffered horrendous things in their early days. One of the ladies with whom I spent several hours had been orphaned as a baby and had been brought up in an orphanage. She had suffered terrible deprivation in every aspect of her life. She was utterly devoid of parental love. For a considerable time she sat between my husband and myself; the only words that came from her lips were, "Mamma, Papa," as we cradled her in our arms. It seemed that as our arms were around her, God was touching deeply into her buried pain, and pouring into her His own restoring love. As this lady chose to forgive those who had neglected, misused and abused her, she was enfolded into the Father heart of God as He revealed Himself to her.

Lives sometimes need remaking

The God who designed and made us so wonderfully is the one who knows us as we are. He is the only one who can remake and reshape us into His original plan.

In the middle of trouble and despair, Job felt deserted by God. In Job 10:8–12, he reminds God of His personal care in creating him and sustaining him. He also questions God and wants to know how God, who so wonderfully formed him in the womb, could let so much evil befall him.

Job goes back to his beginning. He sees God as a potter shaping him from a lump of clay.

> *Your hands shaped me and made me ... Remember that you molded me like clay ... [You clothed] me with skin and flesh and knit me together ... You gave me life ... and in your providence watched over my spirit.*

Fearfully and wonderfully made, yet life didn't make sense.

The potter and the clay

In Jeremiah 18:1–6 we read of Jeremiah going down to the house of the potter because God told him to go. He watched the potter working at the wheel and saw that the pot was marred in his hands. With his strong hands, the potter reshaped the pot, reforming it in the way that he saw best.

God was speaking to Israel. The message given to Jeremiah in the potter's house was that God is like the potter. As the potter reshapes the clay in his hands, so God will do that with His people. There was something wrong with the clay, not with the potter. The misshaped pot was not discarded – it was reshaped according to the potter's plan after it had been refined. The potter could not reshape a hard piece of clay. It had to be pliable in his hands, soft and yielding.

One evening at Ellel Grange I was about to begin an evening's teaching when someone from the office handed me a message which had been sent by one of our intercessors in the south of England. It read something like this: "There are those among you who are like broken pots. Jesus came to bind up the broken-hearted and to reshape broken lives." Very brief, but a word from God for several of those present. Because it was God's word, the Holy Spirit came in power and God began the remaking process and revealed His heart for His children. The following day a lady gave testimony to what had happened in her life. She had first met her own father in prison when she was four years old, and she had only seen him intermittently since then. Her concept of fathering was negative to say the least, and her sense of abandonment and rejection went deep. She had tried to fill the empty father-hole in ungodly ways, and this had only added to her pain. She saw herself as one of the broken pots, and surrendered herself to the heavenly Potter. In an amazing way, she had a revelation of the Father heart of God for her. She concluded her testimony with the words: "I now have a perfect Father." No person is too broken for Him to restore. In one sense we are all a bit like broken pots. Some people know they are and others don't.

The Potter is your Father

The Potter who creates life and reshapes broken lives is in fact the Father of us all.

> *Yet, O LORD, you are our Father. We are the clay, you are the potter; we are all the work of your hand.*
>
> (Isaiah 64:8)

He formed us. He knows how we are made. He understands us and has compassion on us. Even if earthly parents disown us, He will still be our Father. He has promised never to leave us nor forsake us. The Lord *"is like a father to his children, tender and compassionate to those who fear him"* (Psalm 103:13 NLT). He makes allowances for our weaknesses and does not condemn us when we get things wrong. God has revealed Himself to us as Father and nothing can separate us from His love. As Father He enfolds us, and as Potter He remolds us. We can be assured that He desires our good and He has promised, *"I will guide you along the best pathway for your life. I will advise you and watch over you"* (Psalm 32:8 NLT).

Stepping Stone 4

Do you recognize unmet needs in your life? Can you see yourself as clay in the Potter's hand? Are you willing for Him to remold and reshape you as He knows best?

CHAPTER

5

Child or Slave?

In every human heart there is an inborn need to belong. Ideally the family is the place for this *need* to be met. The reality is that you may not have received this security in your family. Consequently you may experience an ongoing sense of aloneness and anxiety. It is only in relationship with others that we find our true identity. When you come to know God as your Father, through faith in the saving work of the Lord Jesus, you immediately belong to the family of God. In relationship with your heavenly Father and others of His children, your need to belong will be met. Children of God are individually unique and precious, but they all belong to the same family – the family of God.

God has no grandchildren

God only has children; He has no grandchildren, and only His children can truly call Him "Father." It is not uncommon to meet people who think they are in the family of God because they were born into a Christian family, or because they go to church and do many good works. Such people struggle because they do not have a living relationship with Jesus, and God seems distant and unknowable.

Others struggle because they had what we might call a bad birth into the Kingdom. They wonder, are they saved or are they not saved, because they do not seem to have new life in them. Often the problem is that the reality of what Jesus did on the cross for them has not been appropriated. They have not fully applied it to their own lives. They used their will to make some sort of decision, but true repentance and forgiveness were not part of their experience. Consequently, they are trying to build a new life without a proper foundation in place.

How can I be sure that I am a child of God?

The Bible sometimes uses imagery to present truths. We need to understand these truths in order to be sure of our salvation and to live in the fullness of what it means to be a child of God.

1. Our condition before God

The Bible speaks of being **born again**. The Gospel of John talks about those to whom Christ gave power to become children of God. They were *"born not of natural descent, nor of human decision or a husband's will, but born of God"* (John 1:12–13). This Scripture makes it clear that children of God are those who are born of God, and our human will does not bring about this kind of birth. Just as we did not choose to be born physically, so we did not choose to be born spiritually – it is a sovereign work of God. In this process our human spirit, which has been alive since conception, but dead to God, becomes alive to God. God puts His own life into us. We hear the good news of the gospel, God speaks to us, and as we respond in faith, we are born again.

When we are born again there is a change in our condition before God. We are given new spiritual life within. We are made spiritually alive, able to relate to God in prayer and worship and to receive His Word with receptive hearts. The evidence that this is a reality in an individual is a change in nature and behavior.

2. Our position before God

The Bible speaks of being **justified**. This word is used over twenty times in the New Testament. To be justified means to be declared righteous, and it describes what happens when someone believes in Jesus Christ as Savior and Lord. God declares that the person who believes is not guilty, but righteous. It is a legal declaration by God because Christ died to pay the penalty for our sin and lived a life of perfect righteousness. His perfection can be given to every one who trusts in Christ.

> *For all have sinned and fall short of the glory of God, and are justified freely by his grace through the redemption that came by Christ Jesus.*
>
> (Romans 3:23–24)

In justification God changes our legal standing before Him. Our position before God is one of righteousness. There is no condemnation because God sees Christ's righteousness as belonging to us.

3. Our relationship with God

The Bible also speaks of being **adopted** into God's family. A good definition of adoption is "an act of God whereby He makes us members of His family." Adoption has to do with our relationship with God as Father. Through adoption we are called children of God.

> *How great is the love the Father has lavished on us, that we should be called children of God! And that is what we are!*
>
> (1 John 3:1)

We are able to relate to God as Father – as a good and loving Father.

Before we knew God, the Bible says we were children of our father the devil (John 8:44; see 1 John 3:8). We were slaves to sin. On being adopted into God's family, we "*are no longer slaves, but God's children; and since [we] are his children, he has made [us] also heirs*" (Galatians 4:7 TNIV). So now we do not relate to God in the way that a slave relates to their master, but we relate to God in the way that a son or daughter relates to a good father. This most intimate way of relating to God is the doorway to other blessings in our Christian life. From this standpoint we can see God as He really is. We know that He will take care of all our needs (Matthew 6:32). We recognize that as a Father He has compassion on His children (Psalm 103:13). In His role as Father He gives us many good gifts. He gives us the great gift of the Holy Spirit to comfort us and to empower us to live lives worthy of Him (Luke 11:13).

A closer look into adoption

At our new birth, we receive new spiritual life within which is from God, and we are taken into His family. When He justifies us, our fear of Him goes because He makes us right with Him. The demands of the law have been satisfied in Christ and we are righteous before God. Adoption is about warm relationship with God as Father. It is through the experience and blessing of this intimate relationship that we are enabled to live as dearly loved children of a perfect Father.

We might say that being born again and justified have to do with our eternal destination. Adoption is about relationship with God as Father, and it has to do with how we live here and now. It also speaks of our relationships with others of the same family, with all those who can pray, "Our Father in heaven."

We were chosen for adoption

> *For he chose us in him [Christ] before the creation of the world to be holy and blameless in his sight. In love he predestined us for adoption to sonship through Jesus Christ, in accordance with his pleasure and will.*
>
> (Ephesians 1:4–5 TNIV)

Paul is saying that before the creation of the world, God chose those He would adopt into His family to be His children. The purpose for which He chose us was to be like Himself – holy and blameless. The Greek word for "adoption to sonship" is a legal term referring to the full legal standing of an adopted male heir in Roman culture. Succession in a Roman family always went down the male line, therefore the male gender is used here to describe us all.

Once adopted we are free from slavery

> *The Spirit you received does not make you slaves, so that you live in fear again; rather, the Spirit you received brought about your adoption to sonship. And by him we cry, "Abba, Father." The Spirit himself testifies with our spirit that we are God's children.*
>
> (Romans 8:15–16 TNIV)

This Scripture makes it clear that fear belongs to slavery, while intimacy with God belongs to being His child. On being adopted into the family of God, the believer receives the indwelling Holy Spirit (Romans 8:9) and has the most intimate of relationships with our heavenly Father. *Abba* is the intimate Aramaic word for Father. It is not a childlike word. It is a relational word. The children of the family would call the father of the family *Abba* from when they were first able to talk, until the father died. Paul is saying to the Roman believers that we are God's children, and therefore intimately related to Him in the new family to which we now belong.

Adoption in the Roman world

In British culture today, adoption is not necessarily seen as an act of love. To understand the life-changing truth of adoption in Scripture we need to understand the background to the New Testament world.[1]

In ancient Rome, adoption was common. And not only were children adopted; grown adults were also adopted. Families could choose to pass on the family name and fortune to someone who was not a blood relation of theirs. Under Roman law, adoption was a serious step and it was not uncommon. Adoption was also commonly used with slaves. Couples who had no children of their own would often select a household slave to adopt, in order to carry on the family name. The adoption process, which was carried out in the presence of seven witnesses, had two steps. The first step was a symbolic sale. The birth father of the boy being adopted would sell his son to the adopting father and then buy him back again twice. The third time he did not buy him back, and the son of a slave then belonged to a new father. However, this had to be made legal, and a second ceremony followed where the adopting father went to a Roman magistrate and presented a legal case for the person to be adopted to be transferred to his authority and family. The magistrate would declare to the adopting father, "This boy is now your adopted son," and to the adopted slave he would declare, "You are now the adopted son of your father." With this the adoption ceremony was completed.

This was only the beginning. It would take a lifetime for

1. For this information I am grateful to William Barclay, *The Daily Study Bible* , "The Letter to the Romans" (Edinburgh: St. Andrew's Press, 1975), pp. 105–106.

the relationship of father–child to grow and mature. A true understanding of adoption gives to us an overwhelming sense of permanence. God's relationship with His children is permanent. As His child, whatever you do, you cannot cease to be adopted, and He will never cease to seek to win your love. God's character and purposes never change because He is unchanging.

The consequences of adoption

Under Roman law there were consequences for the one being adopted. Similarly there are real consequences for us when we are spiritually adopted.

a. The adopted person was chosen, and in that choice got a new father. In this new family he gained all the rights of a son born into the family. It is the same for the believer. The new Father, who chooses each child to draw into His new family, is the perfect Father. In the new family, it is not fear that reigns but undeserved unconditional love.

b. The relationship could not be broken. The adopted person became heir to all that his father owned. Even if other sons were later born into the family, it did not alter his rights. They were secured through adoption. This is the meaning behind Galatians 4:7:

> *So you are no longer slaves, but God's children; and since you are his children, he has made you also his heirs.*
>
> (TNIV)

There is a change of status. From slavery to sonship through God's grace, and therefore an heir of all the rights, privileges and blessings which come to us through Christ Jesus.

c. In law the old life of the adopted person was behind him. He was dead to his past life and alive to his new life in his new family. If he owed anyone anything, all his debts were wiped out. His past life was behind him and the new life was before him. Similarly the Christian is reckoned as dead to the old life (Romans 6:11). The debt has been paid and he or she is free to live a new life with their adoptive Father.

Adoption, then, was a powerful social practice by which a family chose to include someone as a member of that family with all the rights, privileges and blessings. And it was something commonly used with slaves.

Instead of God acting toward you like an angry master, God has adopted you into His own family. So isn't it wonderful news to hear that you have been adopted as a child of God?

Joan's story

Joan was adopted as a very young baby. Her birth parents already had six children and definitely did not want another child. A childless couple lived within sight of the home where this large family was based. In an unusual gesture, Joan's mother knocked on the couple's door and asked, would they like to adopt a baby? As soon as Joan was born she was put into the care of this couple and eventually adopted. From a young age she knew her history, and from childhood to teenage years she observed "the other family." When I met Joan she was a beautiful woman in her late thirties. Her gratitude to her adoptive parents was deep. She had been dearly loved and accepted, and received a quality of life she could never have known in her birth family. As an adult she was able to see what she had been rescued from.

Joan's is an unusual story for someone adopted. She was secure in her identity and did not have deep rejection issues, which often appear in adopted children. Her story illustrates what happens in the lives of God's adopted children.

Firstly, she had evidence to prove her adoption in the form of legal adoption papers provided by the court of law. Secondly, there was the evidence of her own heart – the deep knowing that she was unconditionally loved, accepted and nurtured by parents who had chosen to make her their very own child.

Similarly, God's children have two-fold evidence to prove their adoption. Firstly, they have the evidence of the Word of God. We may parallel this to the legal adoption papers. This evidence can never be discredited or annulled. It stands for eternity. Secondly, there is the evidence of the heart. The deep inner knowing, the Holy Spirit impacting our human spirit with the assurance that we are no longer slaves but God's very own children; His treasured possession, unconditionally loved and unconditionally accepted by a Father who will never let us go.

As a perfect Father, God will never cast off His children. His love does not depend on performance or attainment. He will go out of His way for His children to feel His love for them. So why are there so many aching hearts for a deeper revelation of His presence and love? What stands in the way of this wonderful relationship being according to the desire of our Father's heart? The following are life issues which many people have to deal with for a closer walk with God.

1. Roots

The whole of life is influenced by what has gone before. To enter into our inheritance as adopted children, we will have to address our past. We can no more detach the present from the past than a tree can walk away from its roots. Wounds from the past cause present pain – wounds inflicted by parents, authority figures and other people who have influenced our formative years.

It is not uncommon for people to say, "I feel as though I'm

adopted." They are saying that they do not feel they really belong. They say it because they feel confused as to who they are, and they often have a sense of inner loneliness. Wounds causing such inner pain are deep wounds. Sometimes it takes time to get to the deep place because it is difficult to face pain that has been long buried. Facing hidden issues of the past is a journey of restoration, however painful it may be. Wounds cause us to live in the past although we are free. They keep us locked in old behavior patterns which are ungodly.

The story is told of a so-called Hindu holy man who, on one occasion when visiting a market in Tibet, saw a dozen or so quail tied by a piece of string to a maypole-like contraption. The quail walked round and round in circles. The man felt compassion for them and paid the owner the price to them set free. The strings attaching each bird to the maypole were cut. But although they were free, the birds continued to walk round and round exactly as they did before the price for their freedom had been paid.

Many people are in that position spiritually. Jesus has paid the price to set them free, but they are bound to the old way of life, gripped by wrong beliefs and mindsets and patterns of behavior which block their way into *"the glorious freedom of the children of God"* (Romans 8:21). Are your roots still holding you?

2. Lies

A wound causes a lie to be planted in the heart. That lie becomes a core belief. A core belief is a belief that affects how you see God, yourself and life. They are called core beliefs because they are so deeply entrenched in us. A core belief can develop into a whole belief system. If our belief system is distorted, we will have a distorted view of truth so that a lie is believed to be truth. Lies are rooted in wounds, and wounds are in the human heart. To see God, ourselves and life from God's perspective involves recognizing the lie, owning the wound in which it is rooted, and receiving healing for our pain.

One incident can cause enormous damage. A child of seven was devastated when her mother left the family home. From that experience she concluded, "Mummy doesn't love me." In time she progressed from believing Mummy didn't love her into the belief, "No one loves me." That of course included people who really did love her, and also God. The wound was deep. The lie was deeply embedded, and though she was God's child she did not consider herself loved by Him.

3. Legalism

Legalism is the opposite of grace. Grace is God giving to us the things we could never earn or deserve. Legalists are the opposite – they follow laws, striving to be better. They feel they earn God's approval by what they do or do not do. As a result, they miss the key to intimacy with Him. Children brought up in families with legalistic beliefs are usually taught to see everything in black or white with nothing in between. Many suffer from false guilt.

Legalism is one of Satan's ploys to keep God's children from the joy of knowing His heart. It is usually accompanied by unwritten rules of things you can do and things you can't do. The Bible is often taken absolutely literally in inappropriate ways, and it is used only as a law book rather than as a love story through which God, in the person of Jesus, has revealed Himself to humankind.

This is how it was in one of the churches where I was nurtured. Unless you toed the party line, you were not accepted. In early adult life it seemed to me that the unwritten motto was, "We do not do emotions." As I have grown in understanding I can see how depression in the lives of some members was a common factor, rooted in the common failure to live up to the "rules."

The joy of knowing this wonderful Father is not through endless activity, trying harder, getting all the rules right and trying to please Him. These things are all our own effort. Jesus, *"who is nearest to the Father's heart ... has made him known"* (John 1:18 NEB). Could legalism be getting between you and God?

4. Habitual sin

Habitual sin keeps people in bondage. They are still living as slaves though they are in reality adopted children – *"people are slaves to whatever has mastered them"* (2 Peter 2:19 TNIV). Christ came to deliver us from slavery.

> *It is for freedom that Christ has set us free. Stand firm, then, and do not let yourselves be burdened again by a yoke of slavery.*
>
> (Galatians 5:1)

Habitual sin, which is usually addiction, locks you into slavery. Whatever the addiction, Jesus came to release the captives. But God never overrides your free will, so captives must want to be free. Freedom begins with owning the addiction and learning to hate it. Men and women have come on our course "Steps to Freedom from Addiction," and many have been set free. Some, however, haven't really wanted to be free because deep down they love the addiction.

For most people, freedom from addiction is a journey – a journey of healing from deep wounds in the heart, and of knowing God. To be free you must desire to be free. You must also recognize that you cannot walk in isolation but that you need someone more mature than yourself to whom you can be accountable.

5. Fear of rejection

Fear of rejection is a major fear and it hinders all relationships. Fear of rejection is the result of having been rejected at vulnerable times in our life. Rejection has been called "The Devil's Masterpiece." Whether the rejection was real or perceived, it can rob Jesus Christ of His rightful lordship in a life, and rob God's children of the security of His love.

Rejection is one of the deepest wounds a human being can experience. The wounds of rejection touch deep into the human heart with unbearable pain. Feelings of rejection cause us to feel of little value, unworthy, useless, unsatisfactory and unwanted. Fear of rejection takes us into isolation. We reject other people so that we will not be rejected, and we give the impression that we don't want anyone near. The inside story is quite different. There is a longing to be involved, to be loved and valued, and to have meaningful relationships.

The saddest aspect of fear of rejection is that we believe we are unacceptable to God. We are believers, we know that we are saved, Jesus is our Savior, but despite that, we do not know the compassionate heart of God. Jesus went to the cross so He could replace our fear of rejection with the unconditional acceptance and love of God. Could this be an issue that affects your relationship with God?

Liz's story

Liz had been a Christian since her early teens, and had many ups and downs since. She was the middle child of three girls, and was thirteen months younger than the firstborn. Liz, who is quite short in height, was always compared with her two tall sisters. As a child she felt she was the least favored, and was the unseen member of her family. Her sisters made their presence felt, so she kept quiet.

When I met Liz she said she was "into a season of weeping." Facebook had become an escape route from her pain, but it proved to reinforce rather than relieve it. She had found people from the past, but it seemed they didn't want to stay in touch after the initial contact. Her emotions were in turmoil. She had received previous ministry for trauma – could some of the trauma still be hidden, and was that why she felt no contact with God?

We were led to pray into her loneliness, and very strong emotion began to surface. She told us that she had never been able to bond with her mother, and when she was very young her father, an angry man, had left home. It became clear during our time of prayer as the Holy Spirit took Liz into the source of her fear of rejection, that she had been rejected from conception. In the womb she was neither welcomed nor affirmed, and had been affected by the anger her father had vented on her mother. She had taken into her spirit her mother's pain.

We prayed into Liz's anxiety as a result of not being bonded to her mother. This was painful for her, but it was also healing and restoring. She was able to offer true forgiveness to her mother. The father wounds were deeper than the mother wounds. There were issues of abandonment, isolation and severe rejection. As we prayed for Liz, she felt held in her heavenly Father's arms. The process of healing her broken heart became reality as God revealed to her His Father heart. Revelation is for transformation. As God revealed Himself to Liz, the father wounds of rejection, which had led to a lifetime of fear and rejection, were touched by the healing presence of God.

You are no longer slaves, but God's children

> *So you are no longer slaves, but God's children; and since you are his children, he has made you also heirs.*
>
> (Galatians 4:7 TNIV)

This is the truth. Our position as God's adopted children does not depend on our feelings. The relationship is an enduring one that will last for ever. God never rejects His children, even if they act like slaves. Our heavenly Father's intention is for His children to know His love for them and, as the perfect Father, He has done all that is necessary for that to become reality.

Stepping Stone 5

Are you living in the freedom of knowing you are Father God's adopted child? Do you need to face issues in your past which keep you in slavery?

CHAPTER 6

Keys to Knowing God

Many people seek healing, but healing can never be a means in itself. If healing does not lead to an enriched relationship with God through the person of Jesus Christ, we have to question the validity of that healing. Healing and knowing God cannot be separated. True healing brings change in your life – a change above all else in focus, attitude to God, desire for God, and eagerness to please Him. We can spend our lives seeking healing instead of seeking after God.

I believe there are three prime keys to knowing God and to receiving healing – the lordship of Jesus Christ in our life, forgiveness of other people and acceptance of ourselves. If the first key is not used, the other two won't fit the lock. When Jesus Christ is truly Lord in our life, we receive enabling grace to forgive those who have offended or wounded us, and to accept ourselves as we are.

Key 1: The lordship of Jesus

God's relationship with His people is always a covenant relationship. A covenant relationship is one based on solemn promises. We looked at adoption in the last chapter. That is a relationship of promise – God will be our father, and we will be His children. When we are adopted in the family of God we are in covenant relationship with Him. According to the Roman-Syrian law book, a father might be able to disown his biological son if he had good reasons, but because adoption is entering into a covenant, he could never disown his adopted son. The analogy of adoption which the Bible uses is a very strong one indeed. It gives an overwhelming sense of God's permanent relationship with His children. Our side of the covenant relationship is to make Jesus Christ our Lord.

> *If you confess with your mouth, "Jesus is Lord," and believe in your heart that God raised him from the dead, you will be saved. For it is with your heart that you believe and are justified, and it is with your mouth that you confess and are saved.*
>
> (Romans 10:9–10)

To confess means to agree with God and to live out what you have said.

BEN'S STORY

Ben was a hardened man of the world. Persuaded by his wife, he arrived at our church one Sunday evening. As he listened to the message, he was overcome with grief as he recognized what Jesus had done on the cross that he might be forgiven. At the end of the service he told me that he wanted to be saved, and I pointed him to the verses above in Romans, asking him to read them out loud. The words "Jesus is Lord" would not come out of his mouth. They stuck in his throat and he went away without being saved. The next Sunday the same thing happened. At this time neither my husband nor I had experience in the ministry of healing and deliverance, but we found a couple in the city where we lived who had been missionaries and were willing to help.

Ben was born to military parents in India, and was brought up by a Hindu nanny. As a tiny baby she had dedicated him to a Hindu god. In his lifelong search for truth, Ben had gone along many wrong paths. As the missionaries prayed for Ben, he was delivered from the strongholds of Satan, the curse of idolatry was broken over his life, and with deep brokenness and humility he declared "Jesus is Lord." Jesus became his Savior and his Lord, and Ben was adopted into the family of God.

LORDSHIP AND COVENANT

To understand lordship, we need to understand a little of the nature of covenant. In the Old Testament the Lord adopted Israel as His people, and agreed that He would be their God. The people entered into covenant relationship by making promises of obedience. The terms of the old covenant were written on stone in the form of the Ten Commandments. In Exodus 24, Moses told the people the words and laws which God had spoken. They responded with one voice: "*Everything the LORD has said we will do*" (v. 3).

Following the agreement, young bulls were offered to the Lord. Moses caught the blood in a bowl. He sprinkled half of the blood on the altar, and sprinkled the other half upon the people with the words: "*This is the blood of the covenant that the LORD has made with you*" (v. 8). The people responded a second time: "*We will do everything the LORD has said; we will obey*" (v. 7). The covenant was sealed with blood. Despite Israel's rebellion and repeated breaking of their side of the covenant, it could never be taken away or annulled. Once given, because God is God – holy, just and righteous – He could never break the covenant.

The old covenant, written on tablets of stone and sealed by the blood of animals, could never change people's hearts. So hundreds of years later, God made a promise through His prophets that He would make a new covenant which He would write on people's hearts.

> *I will put my law in their minds and write it on their hearts. I will be their God, and they will be my people.*
>
> (Jeremiah 31:33)

The promised new covenant would change people from the inside out and they would be enabled to love and obey God.

> *I will give you a new heart and put a new spirit in you; I will remove from you your heart of stone and give you a heart of flesh. And I will put my Spirit in you and move you to follow my decrees and be careful to keep my laws.*
>
> (Ezekiel 36:26–27)

During the last evening of Jesus' life, in the upper room with His disciples after the Passover supper, "*... he took the cup, saying, 'This cup is the new covenant in my blood, which is poured out for you'*" (Luke 22:20). The new covenant was sealed with the blood of Jesus. Both the old and the new covenants were sealed with blood. The terms of the old covenant were obedience to the Law. The terms of the new covenant are making Jesus Christ Lord and living out that agreement. The lordship of Jesus Christ is a theme of the New Testament. When Peter preached his first sermon on the day of Pentecost he said to the crowds: "*God has made this Jesus, whom you crucified, both Lord and Christ*" (Acts 2:36). Paul wrote to the Philippians that one day

> *... at the name of Jesus every knee should bow ... and every tongue confess that Jesus Christ is Lord, to the glory of God the Father.*
>
> (Philippians 2:10–11)

To be in the new covenant is to be in the family of God, which means to acknowledge by word and by life that Jesus Christ, who is Lord of all, is my Lord and my God.

Whenever I have taught on the Father heart of God, before praying for the people present to have a meeting with God and a revelation of His heart for them, I emphasize the importance of the lordship of Jesus, and I lead them in the following prayer. Perhaps you would like to pray it also.

Lord Jesus Christ, I acknowledge my need of You and accept You as my Savior and my Lord. I choose now to make You Lord of the whole of my life.

Lord of my spirit and all my worship.
Lord of my mind, my attitudes, and my thinking.
Lord of my feelings, and my expression of emotion.
Lord of my will, and all my decisions.
Lord of my body, and my physical health.
Lord of my sexuality, and its expression.
Lord of my past, my present, and my future.
Lord of my death, and its timing.
Lord of my family, and all my relationships.

I bow my knee and proclaim that Jesus Christ, who is Lord of all, is my Lord and my God to the glory of God the Father.

It is easy to say the prayer from the head through the lips, but Jesus is crowned Lord in our hearts. Imagine that there is a throne in your heart, and there are three types of heart. There are three possibilities. There is the heart where self is enthroned. There is the heart where Jesus is enthroned. Then there is the divided heart where a person thinks that the selfish I can share the throne with Jesus.

THE SPIRIT THAT IS AGAINST JESUS

On one occasion, as I was leading the people in the lordship prayer at Ellel Grange, I noticed a man whose countenance became dark. As the prayer continued he became angry, and as I began to minister the restoring love of God, he ran from the room. Something inside the man could not be in a place where Jesus was upheld as Lord. In his pre-Christian life this man had been in a rock group where he had sung words addressed to antichrist. When the strong spirit of antichrist was cast out of the man, his whole countenance changed. He proclaimed Jesus as his Lord, and for the first time in his life he was able to grasp the personal love of God.

JESUS IS LORD OF ALL OR HE IS NOT LORD AT ALL

The throne of the heart is only big enough for one person. Jesus is Lord of all or He is not Lord at all. If He is not all in all to us, we will have to look for affection elsewhere, because the heart is made for love. We have a God-shaped hole that can never be filled with human love.

The turning point in the lives of many people comes when they see the implications of their choice to crown Jesus Lord of their lives. This brings great delight to the Father's heart. When Jesus was preparing His disciples for His death on the cross and His departure from the world, they were sorrowful. His words of comfort to them were: "*... the Father himself loves you because you have loved me and have believed that I came from God*" (John 16:27).

Those who love Jesus – and to love Jesus means to make Him Lord of all and live in obedience to Him – have that unique sense of knowing that they are loved by the Father. Since Jesus is equal with the Father (John 10:30), He knows the very heart of the Father. It is a heart of truth and love. Jesus shows us the heart of the Father, and draws us closer to His love.

Key 2: Forgiving others

Forgiveness is at the heart of the Bible, and it is the heart of the gospel. Forgiveness is the reason why Jesus came. He came that we might receive forgiveness of sins and the gift of the Holy Spirit (Acts 2:38). None of us could ever earn God's forgiveness, and we certainly could never deserve it. It is a gift of God's grace, the gateway into the Kingdom of God, and the ultimate truth of how dearly we are loved by God.

This is how God showed his love among us: He sent his one and only Son into the world that we might live through him.

(1 John 4:9)

Forgiving others is a major issue for countless people. The truth is that unless we do forgive, we are separated from the intimacy of God's presence. True heartfelt forgiveness to others is only possible when we have received forgiveness ourselves from God. Deep forgiveness from God for our own sin softens our hardened hearts, and enables us to see more clearly from His perspective.

Forgiving others is a major key to healing. The world has recognized the dangers of unforgiveness. In 2001 perhaps the world's first secular forgiveness course was held at Leeds University, led by a Dr Ken Hart. The course delegates ranged from victims of burglary, jilted husbands, the bullied, abused, neglected, abandoned and betrayed. They were all angry and bitter, wanting revenge. The *Daily Telegraph* review heading read, "Holding a grudge can hold you back and damage your health." For the believer, holding a grudge and failing to forgive certainly holds us back from a deepening relationship with God. It damages our spiritual health, and often our physical health also.

A pastor's wife accompanied her husband on one of our longer schools. Her reason for coming was to receive healing for her multiple physical symptoms. She was barely coping with everyday life, was in considerable pain and on a very restricted diet. On the first occasion she received personal prayer she related her story of the desperate situation that had developed in the church, and her fear of a church split.

To forgive the people concerned was not initially on her agenda, but as she allowed God to get her in touch with her deeply buried emotions, she made the choice to forgive each person for what they had done. The process took two or three hours as her well of pain opened and overflowed. Five days later, after we had celebrated communion, the lady asked if she could share what God had done in her life. In a few sentences she told how she had chosen to forgive those who had deeply wronged her husband and spoken ill of her, and how that process had brought her complete physical healing. From that time she had experienced no more pain or discomfort, and she had eaten everything put before her with no ill effects.

To forgive is not cheap. It can be extremely costly, but so was our forgiveness from God. We have all been wounded, but some people have suffered in ways that seem beyond human endurance, and they have much to forgive. However deeply someone has been wounded, they will have to reach the place of forgiveness if they are to be close to God.

FORGIVE US OUR DEBTS AS WE HAVE FORGIVEN OUR DEBTORS

The prayer that we know as "The Lord's Prayer" in Matthew 6:9–13 is a pattern of prayer for believers who have already received forgiveness for their sins. It is a prayer for those who belong to the Father because it begins with, "Our Father." The words *"Forgive us our debts, as we also have forgiven our debtors"* doesn't imply that forgiveness for our sins is in proportion to us forgiving the sins of others against us. If that were so, forgiveness would no longer be of grace – it would be earned.

The prayer assumes two things. Firstly, people have hurt us. Secondly, we have hurt God. Jesus did say immediately afterwards, *"if you forgive men when they sin against you, your heavenly Father will also forgive you. But if you do not forgive men their sins, your Father will not forgive your sins"* (Matthew 6:14–15). These verses state that if we forgive others the Father will forgive us. This doesn't mean that forgiveness of others earns us the right to be forgiven – it means that God only forgives those who are truly sorry for their sins, those who have truly been repentant. One of the chief evidences of true repentance is a forgiving spirit. If we do not forgive, we become obsessed with self, and self-pity replaces our God-given capacity to love Him and others. We become hard on the inside, losing the relationship of intimacy with Jesus and the experience of living in the Father's love.

FORGIVENESS IS A JOURNEY

For many people, forgiveness is a journey. Every journey begins with a single step. The first step in the journey is always the step of choice. Forgiveness needs to be specific. Blanket forgiveness is not "real." True forgiveness involves going into a depth of pain that you do not know you have. It may mean grieving for what you have lost. Acknowledging that the devastation is deeper than you thought it was. When you have truly forgiven, you are at peace with yourself and with God.

A lady who had done one of our longer schools had received considerable ministry, and it was time to go home. She lingered after others had gone, and told me her great disappointment was that she felt no closer to God. She still had the gap between head and heart. She told me of her struggle to forgive her father who had sexually abused her. She had forgiven him many times for abusing her, and she was sincere. Two main consequences of this abuse were loss of her childhood, and loss of any sexual joy in her marriage. She specifically forgave her father for these two things, and deep grief came from her inner being. I prayed that God would reveal His Father heart to her, and bring joy into her marriage. When I met this lady again several months later, her husband had sent her with a message of thanks. He now had a wife. When God is allowed to do deep things, He never forgets to reward.

The certain thing is that one who forgives and lives a life of continual forgiveness lives near to the heart of God. The point is that if we truly know God's forgiveness, forgiving others is not optional.

Roy Hession was involved in the Rwandan revival half a century ago. He once told the story of a Rwandan whom God used greatly in the revival. The man was walking up the hill that led to the church one morning when he saw someone walking in front carrying a heavy burden. On catching up with the stranger he saw that it was Jesus. He asked Jesus if the burden he was carrying represented the sins of the world. The reply was, "No, not the sins of the world, just your sins." I guess that godly man didn't struggle with forgiving others.

Key 3: Self-acceptance

Two great needs we all have are the needs for unconditional love and unconditional acceptance. For many of us, the best we receive is conditional love and conditional acceptance; love and acceptance only on the condition that we behave in certain ways. The problem with it is that the message we receive in our hearts is "You yourself are unlovable and you are unacceptable." When we are rejected, or perceive we are being rejected by others, the doorway to self-rejection is opened. Rejection by human fathers is deep rejection, causing wounds in our human spirit. If you feel rejected by your human father, you will struggle to believe that God accepts you unconditionally because of Jesus, once you are in Christ.

Self-rejection is one of the main barriers to wholeness and to knowing the Father's love. Non-acceptance of ourselves ranges from the rejection of some physical aspect of our being to a wholesale rejection or hatred of self. We each need to accept ourselves as the person God made us, unique and precious to Him. To experience inner peace we must accept ourselves as we are, and allow God to change us into the person He originally intended. We are all unique and precious to Him. As we humble ourselves and come to Him as we are, we find Him to be all-sufficient. He forgives our sins, heals our wounds, covers our weaknesses and failures, and redeems the past of which we may be truly ashamed.

Self-rejection, when harbored, grows into self-hatred, making a person wallow in self-pity which gnaws away on the inside.

Self-hatred can be rooted in different things – parental neglect, abuse, or the deprivation of never having been fathered being some of them. Whatever the roots may be, it is important to renounce self-hatred, to come to Jesus for healing of our brokenness, and to receive all that comes to us from His death on the cross. Otherwise we will search for love in other places, causing ultimate heartache.

The prodigal son came to his senses when he was in the pigsty. Full of self-loathing, he made his way home to his father. A pathetic sight, with nothing to offer but his wasted life, he was embraced in his father's loving arms. If you are to know the Father's embrace, you will have to come the same way. Accept that you cannot change yourself, that you are loved and accepted as you are, and acknowledge that the "Father's embrace" is for you personally as one of His children.

Stepping Stone 6

Read the prayer above on the lordship of Jesus. Are there areas of your life where Jesus needs to become Lord? Do you need to forgive others, or yourself?

CHAPTER

7

Guilt, False Guilt, and Shame

A few years ago, at a Christian convention, I attended a seminar on shame. I was amazed to see a very long line of people queuing. The seminar was so oversubscribed that the venue had to be changed to a much larger one, and then repeated. The gist of the teaching was, identify your emotions and beliefs, exchange any lies you believe for truth, and believe who you are in Christ. It was helpful, but my experience tells me that shame is not a superficial issue.

A three-leaf clover

We could say that guilt, false guilt, and shame are like a three-leaf clover. Their roots are in sin. It may be our own sin or it may be sin committed against us. Whether the problem is guilt, false guilt or shame, they affect all aspects of relationship – how we relate to God, how we relate to other people, and how we relate to ourselves.

New creations

On becoming Christians, despite being told, *"if anyone is in Christ, the new creation has come. The old has gone, the new is here!"*

(2 Corinthians 5:17 TNIV), many are still struggling. The Scripture is true, of course. The old has gone because at conversion we turn

> *from darkness to light, and from the power of Satan to God, so that [we] may receive forgiveness of sins and a place among those who are sanctified by faith [in Jesus].*
>
> (Acts 26:18)

New Testament teaching affirms that the old has gone, in that living to please the sinful nature and for self is a thing of the past. The new has come, in that there is a new desire to live by the Spirit and to live for God.

Sanctification is a lifelong process for us all. It is a process of being changed more and more into the likeness of Christ. Dealing with feelings of guilt, false guilt, and shame are part of that process.

Struggling to perform, to please, to do better, to be an overcomer is to try to change oneself. The lie believed long ago, "I'm only loveable for what I do," becomes more deeply embedded. Self-improvement programs are doomed to fail. A fairly recent survey reported that sixty percent of Christians feel guilty for sins committed in the past. Past problems of abuse, addiction, divorce, rejection, and trauma, to name but a few, have a present disturbing effect. Our damaged emotions don't simply disappear when we come to Christ. They are part of the baggage of our old life.

Real guilt

Guilt is an emotion we feel when we know or think we have done something wrong. It is right to feel guilt when we have said, done or even thought wrong. Sin brings guilt. If a person breaks God's laws, goes beyond His boundaries, they are guilty. Guilt has to be paid for. On the cross, Jesus became our guilt offering – He paid for the guilt – so that we can be forgiven and cleansed from sin. As we have seen, the Bible word for this is "justified." This means that God sees the forgiven sinner just as if he or she had never sinned. The sin is dealt with. God will not remember it any more. Forgiveness is complete.

Some sin carries with it deep shame. When this is the case, to be free from shame and to live in the joy of forgiveness, the person needs to confess their sin to another person (in accordance with James 5:16) if they are going to be able to move into freedom and be cleansed from a guilty conscience. The longer a person remains feeling ashamed, the more the roots of shame grow deeper, and the person is haunted by the memory.

Mike's story

Mike came to the Lord in his late thirties. He was brought up without boundaries, and committed deep sin. When he became a Christian he was eager to get rid of his past baggage, and be released from the strongholds of Satan. He received regular ministry, and over a period of a couple of years he was indeed a new creation. He was growing in Christ, and was an effective witness.

Some time later he approached me, and asked me to pray for him. The euphoria following his conversion had waned, and God seemed distant. I asked him if there was anything in his past that he had not brought into the light. His answer was no. When he approached me a second time for prayer, I felt God was showing me Mike's problem – something from years ago which he was deeply ashamed of, and which he needed to own. On his third visit I assured him that it was safe to bring into the light anything, however deeply ashamed he might be. With this he broke down, and confessed the sin that still haunted him from years ago. Mike had to come into the light to be healed from guilt and shame. The sin he had confessed to God countless times was brought into the light, and finally laid to rest.

> *... if we walk in the light, as he is in the light, we have fellowship with one another, and the blood of Jesus, his Son, purifies us from all sin.*
> (1 John 1:7)

False guilt

A person suffers from false guilt when they feel guilty before God and they are not. False guilt is very hard to bear. Satan launches attacks of condemnation so that people do not feel forgiven even after they have repented before God in response to feelings of guilt.

When we feel bad about ourselves, we usually seek to escape this condemnation through self-improvement or self-justification. Symptomatic behavior patterns are adopted which become coping mechanisms to enable us to get on with life. Some of these include self-blame, and taking on other people's burdens. Over-involvement in religious activities, judging others and justifying self. Perfectionism and criticism of others often go hand in hand. Anxiety and stress are part of the false guilt syndrome.

Possible root causes of false guilt

These are many and varied, and often include:

- Lack of freedom in childhood. Too many dos and don'ts
- Being falsely blamed when others are responsible
- Having been sinned against and feeling "It's my fault"
- Critical or overprotective parenting
- Failure or inability to meet parental expectations

- Deprivation, cruelty or neglect
- False responsibilities as a consequence of traumas, accidents or sicknesses
- Abuse – sexual, mental, emotional, physical or spiritual
- Domineering or overbearing authority

Jake's story

Jake lacked intimacy from either of his parents. His mother suffered depression, and his father was given to bouts of anger and withdrawal. Jake was sexually abused by a relative when he was seven years old. He was convinced he was to blame, and although he had brought the abuse to God many times, he still felt guilty. He believed he was a bad person.

Jake knew from Scripture that God is loving and forgiving. If we confess our sin to Him, He will forgive, but he still felt condemned. During a prayer time a memory was stirred, and he remembered words spoken by his father. On one occasion when he had done a childish thing, which brought his parents' disapproval, Jake's father refused to speak to him. When he did speak he said, "I'll forgive you, but I'll never forget." When Jake forgave his father, and the power of the words spoken over him were broken, he moved from the prison of false guilt into freedom.

What is shame?

Shame is harder to bear than guilt. Guilt says, "I made a mistake. I did wrong." Shame says, "I am a mistake. I am wrong." Shame is more than an emotion. It is a mindset. It is a core belief about oneself – "I am a defective person." Deep feelings of being inadequate, incapable, stupid or worthless saturate our being.

Shame is an identity which people can adopt. It covers a person like a cloak, but is not often recognized. Receiving forgiveness from God and extending forgiveness to others releases a person from hatred and shame. The cloak has to be taken off at the cross, and cleansing received.

Shame is associated with exposure. Adam and Eve were ashamed in the garden after they had sinned (Genesis 3:7). We touched on this earlier. Initially they were not aware of their nakedness. Through sin they lost their innocence. They tried to hide from each other and from God by making coverings for themselves.

Their own effort of sewing fig leaves together as a covering was futile. Only God could cover their shame, and for them to be covered, blood had to be shed. *"The LORD God made garments of skin for Adam and his wife and clothed them"* (Genesis 3:21). The blood of animals was shed, and their skins covered the shame of Adam and Eve. They were guilty, and their guilt brought them shame.

Guilt tells us something is bad; shame says, "I am bad"

Guilt involves a confrontation with sinful behaviors. Shame is different. It attacks the identity of a person. When sin is confessed, guilt is removed. But shame "owns" a person and keeps them in bondage. When Lazarus was raised from the dead by Jesus, he was very much alive yet he was bound with heavy grave clothes which were visible (see John 11:43–44). Shame has the same effect as grave clothes – it keeps a person bound, but it is invisible and not as easy to recognize.

Guilt and shame are God-given emotions intended to bring us to repentance. No one knew this more than David who was put to shame by his own sin, and by sin committed against him. He wrote:

> *In you, LORD my God, I put my trust. I trust in you; do not let me be put to shame, nor let my enemies triumph over me. No one who hopes*

in you will ever be put to shame, but shame will come on those who are treacherous without cause.

(Psalm 25:1–3 TNIV)

Shame has to do with exposure

As we have seen, Adam and Eve sewed fig leaves together because they realized they were naked. They were exposed to one another – their nakedness brought a sense of shame. The fresh loveliness of their innocence was replaced by a sense of shame before the Lord who had created them. In their folly they thought the trees of the garden and fig leaves sewn together could hide them from God. When one has a shame-based identity, trying to hide is automatic. The way of healing is the way of openness to God. Since He is omniscient He knows everything, and hiding pushes Him further away.

Consequences of exposure to shame

Shame is the consequence of inner damage. So change has to take place on the inside. Until the wounded emotions are healed, shame does not go away. Inner healing is healing of the wounded emotions that are controlling our present behavior.

The following are some examples of that behavior. They are the "fig leaves" which some of us use to cover up our shame. They are patterns of behavior and lifestyles. These issues bring separation from other people, and also from our heavenly Father.

Denial means to deny the reality of what has happened. We may either deny the real problem, or we may rationalize it in order to make things seem better than they were. We do it to try to minimize pain. Denial serves as a safety barrier to shield us from the reality of the true situation. Broken people have usually been in denial for many years, and denial has become a way of life. Denial also involves making excuses for one's own sin or the sin of others.

Anxiety Many people with anxiety disorders cannot remember a time when they were not given to anxiety. Deep anxiety is frequently the result of not having been protected and bonded with emotionally and physically in babyhood and childhood. Anxiety can go back to experiences in the womb, and can be lodged in the deeper emotions of the human spirit.

Insecurity is a common dilemma. It is often the result of rejection, including rejecting oneself. Someone who felt rejected in their earliest days lacks a sense of being attached to either or both parents. Insecure people sometimes spend their lives trying to be perfect in order to please people. The result is like a hamster on a wheel. They get nowhere.

Isolation Relationships were God's idea. He made us to relate to one another and to Himself. Isolation separates and deprives a person of meaningful relationships. Isolating ourselves helps us to avoid feeling vulnerable, and the fear associated with it. Yet in our hearts there is a cry for love and closeness. We do it to cover shame, and the feelings of inadequacy and inferiority that come with shame.

Failure No one has a record of never having failed, except those who don't do anything! If we do anything in life, we will continue to fail, and continue to pick ourselves up afterwards and go on with life. However, someone with a shame-based identity has an identity of failure, and ceases to pursue their God-given destiny. Destiny is God's plan for your life – the reason why you were born.

Passivity Behind passivity hide feelings of helplessness. The person has given up. We see this in ministry situations when the person expects someone else to do everything for them instead of reaching out to God him or herself. Passivity is an escape world where the person is cut off from pain that they have chosen not to remember. It is a way of trying to cover shame.

Unreality To live in unreality is to live in an unreal world of one's own making in order to avoid pain. Unreality is a world of loneliness because intimate relationships can only exist between real people. Unreality is rooted in shame. The shame of how a person sees themselves, because of the things that have happened to them or from neglect and deprivation.

For Adam and Eve's shame, God made coverings of skins from animals. Their paltry fig leaves were totally inadequate. God has made provision for our deepest shame to be covered and healed. Our heavenly Father does not want shame to separate His children from His love. He gave His only Son for us. Jesus bore our shame that we might be free from its consequences.

Bernard's story

I met Bernard very shortly after he had been asked to leave the church he had pastored. He was overwhelmed with a sense of injustice, convinced he had been wrongly treated. He was an angry man, desiring revenge. It became clear that he had been asked to leave the ministry because he was ministering out of some of the consequences of exposure to shame mentioned above.

Bernard had grown up in the gang culture. He came from a dysfunctional family where he had been abused, neglected and lacked boundaries. He and his brothers were allowed to do as they pleased, with few questions being asked. As a teenager, Bernard committed shameful acts of rebellion, violence and degradation which harmed other people and which left him with a legacy of fear.

In his early twenties Bernard became a Christian, and trained for the ministry. He went into church work with the shame and baggage of the past on his shoulders. He became a disaster in ministry. He was a broken pot needing to be remade in the hands of the heavenly Potter.

Bernard attended one of our long courses. His past was hidden – he had covered it extremely well in Christian circles. For many hours during his ministry sessions he denied his background because he feared exposure. The rebellion of Bernard's past had to be replaced with humility before God, and with complete uncovering of his sin which had caused him so much shame.

Deep sin that causes shame keeps a person in a pit. Some people receiving ministry for shame have had a picture of the hand of Jesus reaching into the pit to lift them out. Some have not found it easy to lift up their hand and place it in the hand of Jesus as an act of faith. They have had to come to the point of saying, "Shame has broken my heart but I have a Savior who is greater than my shame."

Causes of shame

What causes this shame? Firstly, some causes of shame are self-inflicted. Shame is the result of our own sin. It can be the result of the things we have done. Things we may have done many years ago that have not been dealt with at the cross. Secondly, shame can be as a result of the wounding received from others.

Self-inflicted causes of shame

Sin causing shame is usually kept hidden. It may or may not have been done in secret, but it usually involves deception.

Self-inflicted causes of shame are more readily recognized. Forgiveness and cleansing is readily available at the cross. When deep sin which a person is ashamed of has devastated other people, they need to put this right to be healed. Putting things right with those who have been wounded is a step of humility. God always honors humility.

Shame as a result of wounding by others' sinful deeds

People take on themselves the guilt and shame that belong to others. Children who have witnessed parental divorce, imprisonment or suicide by a family member can feel as if they are the guilty party. The following are some of the common causes of wounding by others which cause shame.

ABUSE AND VIOLATION

Children who are abused are the victims. Abuse brings feelings of worthlessness and hopelessness, and a sense of guilt, which is false guilt. The usual cry is, "It must be my fault." It leaves a sense of uncleanness and worthlessness. The accompanying shame usually leads to patterns of behavior which bring more shame – promiscuity, addictions and, like Bernard, crime.

DISAPPOINTMENT OF UNMET NEEDS

These are described in more detail in chapter 4. When our real human needs are unmet, Satan has a chance to play a record in our minds: "There must be something wrong with me if that is how they treat me. Why do they never say anything good to me? Why do they not want me with them? What is wrong with me that they never comfort me or give me a hug?" The longer that message goes on playing, the deeper our shame becomes.

BETRAYAL

Betrayal takes place within relationships. Betrayal is a betrayal of trust. Someone we thought would protect us actually wounds us by words or actions. They seem to go against us. Self-condemnation can set in where the wounded person feels they are to blame for the betrayal.

DISRESPECT

Respect is a top priority emotional need. It is shown through words and actions, as is disrespect. On God's agenda we were each born to receive respect at each stage of development in childhood, and also in adult life. Respect develops significance. Significance says, "I matter, I count, I am worthy, I am affirmed."

Children who live in an environment where significant people respect each other and respect them, grow to feel good about themselves. They are comfortable about who they are. The converse is also true. The opposite environment breeds feelings of insignificance, disrespect and shame.

Summary of the nature of guilt and shame

Guilt is a conviction from the Holy Spirit. Guilt says: "I did wrong, and there is forgiveness for my sin because Jesus died. The arms of my heavenly Father are open wide to me."

Shame brings condemnation. Condemnation comes from others, from self, and from the enemy. Feelings of condemnation bring feelings of isolation from Father God.

Guilt confronts behavior and wrong choices with the truth. "I did wrong, my choices were wrong, but I am not a bad person. I have a Father who loves me unconditionally."

Shame Instead of confronting sin, shame confronts identity.

Shame says, "I am a bad person." The accompanying feelings of hopelessness say, "I can never be any different."

Guilt When the sin behind guilt is owned and confessed, the Holy Spirit brings repentance to the human heart. Confession is to say the same about sin as God says. It is to agree with God. Confession brings peace, the peace of being close to God and loved.

Shame is the companion of despair because shame has to do with secrecy and a failure to bring things into the light.

Shame and sexual sin

Sexual sin is a major source of shame, whether it is personal sexual sin, or having been sinned against sexually. Some people have committed, or had committed against them, grave sexual sin that is not easy to confess to God, let alone to another person. God gave sex as a beautiful gift to be enjoyed in the covenant of marriage that the enemy has distorted. Sexual sin defiles the human spirit, and to be free from the shame that comes with it, the spirit needs to be cleansed by the blood of Jesus.

Shame affects every part of a person

Shame affects every part of a person – body, soul and spirit. Shame profoundly wounds the human spirit. It crushes a person's spirit. The Bible asks the question, *"a crushed spirit who can bear?"* (Proverbs 18:14). It also gives the remedy: *"The LORD is close to the brokenhearted and saves those who are crushed in spirit"* (Psalm 34:18). Because we relate to God and worship Him with our spirit, the wounds of shame on the spirit need to be healed so we grow deeper into the love of our Father in heaven, and grow closer to Jesus.

God's grace and mercy are the only answer for our guilt and shame

God's mercy is never deserved, but He shows us mercy. That is what is so amazing about grace. It is also uncomfortable. We are utterly dependent upon grace and mercy for recovery from guilt and shame.

God's grace and mercy do not depend on our previous behavior, but on personal humbling of ourselves before Him in order to receive. We deserve God's anger against sin and the eternal punishment of separation from Him. But God is merciful and does not give us what we deserve. What's more, He doesn't stop there. In His grace God goes further and actually gives us what we don't deserve – the bountiful outpouring of love, acceptance, forgiveness, and eternal relationship as His sons and daughters.

To be restored from the crippling maladies of guilt and shame we must cast ourselves on God's mercy and grace. He is *"compassionate [merciful] and gracious ... slow to anger, abounding in love ..."* (Exodus 34:6).

The truth sets you free

The truth is the key. Jesus said, *"If you hold to my teaching, you are really my disciples. Then you will know the truth, and the truth will set you free"* (John 8:31–32). Behind shame are the lies of Satan. Lies which feel like truth. As we've already considered, shame is an identity we take on as a result of the things we ourselves have done, or the things other people have done to us. Like a cloak it needs to be taken off, and the wounds underneath the cloak healed by Jesus. Shame is our identity outside of Christ. Our new identity is from knowing who we are in Him. God's children are dearly loved, treasured in His heart:

So near, so very near to God
I cannot nearer be
For in the person of His Son
I am as near as He.

So dear, so very dear to God
More dear I cannot be
The love wherewith He loves His Son
Such is His love to me.

(Catesby Paget)[1]

Healing through the cross

We cannot bypass the cross. It is through the cross, and only through the cross, that we can be free from guilt and condemnation. Free from the shame of the things we have done, and the things done to us. What Jesus did on the cross is more profound than our human minds can take in. When He died on the cross, Jesus was the subject of shame and scoffing. He was dying in the place of each one of us. When He was put to shame, He was taking the sin, shame and degradation of any one of us. Anyone who will receive what He has done and completed.

1. "A Mind at Perfect Peace with God", *Believers Hymn Book*, revised edition (Kilmarnock: John Ritchie Ltd., 1999).

Jesus carried our shame

Isaiah tells us that it was our weaknesses, our sorrows, our troubles, our rebellion and the punishment for our sins that took Jesus to the cross. We were the reason He had to die (see Isaiah 53:3–5).

In Isaiah 53 we have pictures of "the suffering servant." Prophecies written 600 years before Christ, describing crucifixion before crucifixion had even been thought of:

> *... he was pierced for our transgressions ...*
>
> (v. 5)

> *I gave My back to those who struck Me, And My cheeks to those who plucked out the beard; I did not hide My face from shame and spitting*
>
> (Isaiah 50:6 NKJV)

Can you imagine the shame of being crucified naked on a Roman cross in public as a criminal? If shame has to do with exposure, could anyone have been more exposed than the Lord Jesus? The above Scripture describes how hoards of people slapped Him across the face, pulled out the hairs of His beard and spat on Him. He was despised and rejected – He is the helper of the helpless. *"He was whipped so we could be healed"* (Isaiah 53:5 NLT).

The death of Jesus was to bring us to the Father. To break down the barriers which keep us from Him and bring us restoration. There are no quick fixes for shame. Each person must come to the cross and receive the benefits of what Jesus did when He died in their place. That includes you, dear reader.

Fig leaves of shame

When I'm teaching about guilt and shame on an Ellel course,

delegates are invited to become actively involved in a two-stage procedure for addressing issues in their lives.

Firstly, on a cut-out fig leaf, they are asked to write something from their heart regarding their own sense of personal guilt and shame. (Anyone who feels shame also has a problem with guilt, whether real or false.) This first stage usually touches buried emotions, releasing a sense of sorrow.

Secondly, the people are invited to come forward and attach their fig leaves to the cross at the front of the meeting room, if they feel it would be helpful. This is a symbol and a sign that they believe Jesus bore their shame, and that He is able to set them free and heal them, and restore them into their rightful identity in Himself as a child of God.

Whenever this exercise is done, almost every person responds – whether we have large or small numbers of delegates. Some testify that they had never before recognized their shame-based identity, and many testify to a revelation of the Father's heart for them as they are at the cross.

Stepping Stone 7

Imagine you hold a fig leaf in your hand. What would you write regarding any issues of guilt and shame? Turn your thoughts into a prayer, and come as you are to the only One who has the answer to your heart's cry.

CHAPTER 8

Broken Trust and the Faithfulness of God

A young man with high ambitions for his future marriage approached my husband and me one day with a questionnaire. He thought that as we had been married for nearly half a century, we must have some answers as to what keeps a marriage together. His first question was, "What do you consider to be the most important ingredient for a happy marriage?" Without hesitation, David and I simultaneously said, "Trust."

The young man concerned was surprised. He expected us to say that love was the most important quality for a lasting marriage. In one way of course, he was right. Trust cannot really be separated from love. Love and trust are like peas from the same pod. One of the evidences that someone truly loves is that they are trustworthy. Someone who breaks the trust of a person they profess to love does not truly love from the heart.

The importance of trust

We cannot live without trust. From beginning to end the Bible exhorts us to trust God. The reality is that many people find it hard to trust Him despite knowing from Scripture that God is faithful.

Trust in the LORD with all your heart and lean not on your own understanding; in all your ways submit to him, and he will make your paths straight.

(Proverbs 3:5–6 TNIV)

To trust God means to have confidence in His trustworthiness. It means to be secure and safe in Him, and to lean on Him completely. To do this is to submit to God in childlike faith, assured that He is so much wiser and stronger than we are.

Jesus said, *"Do not let your hearts be troubled. Trust in God; trust also in me"* (John 14:1). In John 14, Jesus is telling his disciples of His oneness with the Father and of the eternal home, in which He would prepare a place for them. The word to the disciples is the same word to us. When you trust you are exceedingly safe. It is family trust – those who believe have been adopted into the family for all eternity. The promise of the Father and the Son is unbreakable.

God is trustworthy! For real relationship with Him we will have to trust Him. Similarly, for human relationships to be real and intimate in the way God planned, trust is an important element.

Trust grows from childhood experiences

The ability to trust is learned from our very earliest days –

... you brought me out of the womb; you made me trust in you even at my mother's breast. From birth I was cast upon you; from my mother's womb you have been my God.

(Psalm 22:9–10)

The psalmist is saying that as he was being nurtured at his mother's breast in the safety and security of his mother's arms, he was learning that God is trustworthy. From the very beginning of life he was learning that it is safe to trust – to trust God and others.

Trust is a root emotion we learn as a child

The root emotion of trust learned in childhood comes from the sense of knowing that the people with whom we share our lives can be trusted. A climate of trust is crucial to a child's sense of security and well-being. It brings the assurance that the environment is safe and the child will not be let down.

God's plan

God's plan was that children would grow and develop from a place of safety. He planned for every child to be conceived in love and welcomed into a family where they would receive the unconditional love and acceptance of a father and mother. In such a family a child learns to trust as they are helped to grow and mature within safe boundaries.

In God's plan for families, correction will be fair and just. Fair correction and accountability are character training. In God's plan, mistakes are not punishable offenses, but growing experiences that develop gifting and encourage confidence and risk taking. If this is not the case in our childhood, we may find it difficult in adult life to move out of our comfort zones and trust God.

God intended our knowledge of Him to be gained through godly parenting

Children receive significant messages from their parents through words and actions. When, as children, we are well provided for physically, emotionally and spiritually, we receive the message that we are highly valued. Our deepest needs are met within trusting relationships. We grow in confidence and trust, knowing that to trust those closest to us is safe. When our childhood trust is not broken, we grow up knowing that God is trustworthy, and is worthy of our personal trust.

Similarly, if our parents spend time with us as children and demonstrate faithfulness in marriage, they give us a feeling of security and value. When this is not the case, we may seem fairly resilient on the outside, but on the inside it is different.

One of our grandchildren arrived home from school one day quite tearful, wanting to talk to both of her parents together. Several of her classmates were from broken homes, and this particular day her best friend had said she was very worried because her parents, who were constantly arguing, were thinking of splitting up. Our granddaughter, who was eight when this occurred, needed assurance that this would not happen to her. Her parents assured her that they would always stay together. They said they had made that promise before God, and they would not break their promise. Anna was satisfied. Her parents had never broken a promise, and she had absolute trust in them.

The reality of parenting

The reality of the parenting that we are given as children will affect our inner wholeness, and also our attitudes to God. Over time these attitudes are reinforced, and become firmly held beliefs and attitudes about our heavenly Father and His relationship with His children.

If parents are dismissive, uncommunicative or non-tactile, they are distant parents. Such parents are not easily approached, nor do children usually feel they can trust them with the things that matter.

If parents are neglectful, unaffirming, unpredictable or argumentative, they fail to show tenderness and intimacy. Trust is nurtured within tenderness and intimacy. Children from families where these qualities are not demonstrated find ways to survive, and learn to be independent or self-sufficient. As adults, control becomes a major issue, because it is used to combat insecurity.

Broken trust

A child seems to be born with the innate ability to trust. This is how God designed us to be. However, trust is fragile. Once broken it is not easily restored. Without trust our relationships can never be intimate. More often than not, relationships without trust are built on fear and control.

Trust is a core critical emotion which undergirds all relationships. The quality of our relationship with God and others depends on whether or not we are willing to trust. Trust requires us to be vulnerable. With vulnerability is the risk of being let down and disappointed by those we trust, which means we risk inner wounding.

Trust is broken when others fail in their God-given responsibilities

We have looked at the role of parents in building trust. If we have parents who are unreliable or inconsistent, we feel unsafe. Their behavior gives us the message that they are not dependable. If our parents are moody or unstable we feel insecure. Their inconsistency creates fear in us, and we ask ourselves the question, "Will they accept me or reject me today?" There are, of course, other factors, and in a fallen world unfortunately we have all had our trust broken at some time or other.

Authority figures

People in positions of authority are usually presumed to be trustworthy. They are in fact "father figures" in that they have authority. Children in particular will trust them, occasionally with shattering results.

The school caretaker was responsible for the tuck shop during playtime. He seemed such a kind man, and was especially kind to seven-year-old Janet. Unlike the other children, Janet did not have money to spend at the tuck shop. She always stood alone, envying the other children as they pushed and shoved in the tuck shop queue.

One day the caretaker asked Janet what she would like if she had the money to buy tuck. He said if she would go with him to his office when everyone was served, he would let her choose what she wanted. The sexual abuse went on intermittently for almost a school year with devastating effects. Janet kept "the secret" to herself.

When I met her, she was twenty-two years old and anorexic, engulfed with self-hatred and false guilt. The healing journey for Janet was long and painful and required many hard choices, including the choice to trust her heavenly Father, who would be there in the darkest times.

Spouse's disloyalty

Betrayal is one of the deepest wounds, touching deep into the human spirit. Disloyalty in any relationship is hard to bear. Commitment in relationships is the essence of loyalty. Relationships cannot survive without commitment. Someone who is loyal in a relationship will see the best in the other person. Loyalty says, "I'm here for you when no one else is." "I will always be on your side."

The consequences of misplaced trust can be devastating.

Adultery cannot be called less than betrayal. The person who betrays their spouse sacrifices the trust of their spouse for their own personal ends. The result is that one person is bound to a person they can no longer trust. They are exposed to the possibility of intense hurt.

Our ability to trust is damaged when we perceive that God has let us down

Many people believe God has let them down when things don't go their way. God is absolutely trustworthy, but He does things His way, not as we would like Him to. He is always right, and His ways are always best.

During a session on trust and the faithfulness of God, an agitated lady interrupted the teaching. She was absolutely convinced that God had broken a promise He made to her some twelve years previously. She said she had received a word from the Lord that had not materialized. She had fallen in love with a church leader who was also single, and God had promised this man to her in marriage.

I asked the lady how God had spoken to her. She said words came to her mind and someone else had confirmed the word to her. The man, however, said that God had not given him the same word.

This lady had been in self-deception. What she took as a word from the Lord was nothing more than wishful thinking. Before the course ended, the Holy Spirit spoke to her and brought her to repentance for her heart attitude to God, with a revelation of His true character.

Marry Liz

A man who was locked into an unhappy marriage had married a lady young enough to be his daughter. They both had deep unresolved issues in their lives that aggravated the difficulties in their marriage. This man told me he had married his wife because God had plainly said to him, "Marry Liz." He had married in obedience to the word he heard, but was angry with God and blamed Him for the unhappiness in his marriage.

Like many others, this man had a wrong view of God's character and nature. He was convinced God had planned his marriage, knowing it would not be happy. Father God is a father who delights to give good gifts to His children. He does not plan bad things for His children. When the voice speaking is His voice it is clear and usually confirmed by Scripture.

The man concerned repented for his attitude to God, ceased to blame God. Both the man and his wife were willing to receive help in working through some of their difficulties. They both needed a true revelation of the heart of God for each of them as an individual, and for their relationship together.

Trust involves mind, emotions, and will

Trust is an attitude involving mind, emotions, and will.

With the mind, we conclude that a person is worthy of our trust. It would be foolish to trust someone until they had been proved trustworthy.

With the emotions, we feel trust. We feel the person is reliable and we are prepared to be vulnerable in trusting them, believing they will not take advantage of our openness.

With the will, we practice trust. We make the decision to be open with another person, believing they are dependable and true. To trust is risky, especially when trust has been broken. Therefore, it is always a choice.

Broken trust wounds the human spirit

The victims of broken trust often find it difficult to trust or to be involved in meaningful relationships. Broken trust results in insecurity in their spirit. The human spirit is the most sensitive part of a person. It is like antennae in that it picks up messages that are conveyed by words, actions, attitudes and reactions.

Broken trust crushes the spirit. *"The human spirit can endure in sickness, but a crushed spirit who can bear?"* (Proverbs 18:14 TNIV). In order for us to learn to trust, our spirits must have received messages of truth, assurance, hope, and comfort.

When godly, significant messages are received in the human spirit from childhood, a person will be strong in spirit. We read of both John the Baptist (Luke 1:80) and of the Lord Jesus (Luke 2:40) that *"the Child grew and became strong in spirit"* (NKJV). However, when our spirit is wounded through trust having been broken, the wounds of insecurity from broken trust need to be healed, and our spirit needs to be restored by God.

Jessica's story

We had done a healing weekend in a church, and at the conclusion many people came forward for prayer. Jessica was very distressed as the pastor of the church was commanding an evil spirit to leave her. Some days later, I had a letter from Jessica who said that the pattern was repeated every time she went forward for prayer. She was getting worse instead of better. She felt increasingly abandoned by God.

When I met up with her some weeks later, it was clear that she had a wounded spirit resulting from abandonment and lack of nurture in her earliest days. Her spirit had picked up many wrong messages which deliverance would never rectify. Her need was for a healing touch at the core of her being, and for a revelation of her heavenly Father's love for her. She was able to begin a new journey of healing for her wounded spirit.

Inability to trust others

The inability to trust others is the second consequence of broken trust. A person who has been badly let down will not readily trust again. Unless root issues are dealt with, relationships will never get beyond the superficial, and inner loneliness will be experienced. When trust has been violated, forgiveness is always a big issue. Like trust, forgiveness is a choice we must all make. We make it at the cross where we take our own sins, and the sins done to us.

Bitter root judgments

Bitter root judgments are the consequence of wounding. They are called bitter root judgments because they are rooted in bitterness. The person responds to life in the present out of their past experiences. Bitter root judgments are often made in the foundational years of life. A judgment is a bitter criticism which becomes a generalization, using words like "always," "never" or "typical." They are most likely to be in relation to those close to us, particularly parents and authority figures. These wrong roots in the foundations of our lives cause us to make ungodly judgments against similar people in the present. Though the roots may not be readily recognized in adult life, they are firmly planted in the soil of the heart.

Bitter roots carry with them expectations. If you have a bitter root, you will expect a person in the present to behave in a certain way, and your expectation can subconsciously push that person to behave as expected, even if it is not in that person's will or nature to do so. Bitter root expectations use language like this: "I will be blamed unfairly," "They will not listen to me," "People always reject me," "I'm always treated unfairly," "Never trust a woman," "Men only want one thing."

For example, a young girl discovers that her father is having an affair. She forms the judgment, "You can't trust men; they will always betray you." When she marries, she doesn't trust her husband because of this judgment of long ago. He feels mistrusted and undervalued, and looks for affirmation elsewhere. The woman's belief is reinforced: "I was right. You can't trust men." The principle of sowing and reaping comes into play.

Similarly, a young boy who trusts his mother with his heart feelings is ridiculed and criticized. He forms the judgment, "It's not safe to trust others with what you really think or feel. They will ridicule you or criticize you." When he marries, communication with his wife is poor because he never trusts her with the deeper feelings of his heart. Consequently his wife feels unappreciated and unloved. She thinks, "Surely if you love someone you will trust them." From her hurt she begins to criticize her husband. In turn, he is convinced that his bitter root judgment is right. He doesn't readily see that he is reaping what he has sown.

When you reap what you sow, you don't only reap it once, but many times. Recurrent patterns can give us a clue that there is a bitter root judgment. Suppose you are repeatedly treated unfairly, and you do not see the same happening to other people. You might ask, "Why me?" In this case, it might be that you made a judgment in childhood against someone who treated you unfairly. They were wrong and bad! The bitter root crept in. The expectation grew up, "I am always treated unfairly" and the sowing and reaping began. When we see a repeated pattern in our lives, we should ask God whether there could be a bitter root judgment operating in us.

The remedy for bitter roots

Firstly, we have to see that they are there. We need to recognize the defiling patterns of behavior and relationships that are the fruit of the judgment. For this we will need the help of the Holy Spirit to show us what is hidden in our heart. It may also mean giving others permission to point out what we cannot see for ourselves.

Secondly, it is vital to repent of the specific judgments made in childhood, and to forgive those who have hurt us and caused us to make the judgments. Forgiving them releases us from bitterness so that we no longer project our past pain into present relationships. Forgiveness doesn't necessarily mean the person who has violated our trust is trusted again. It does mean that nursed anger against those who have broken our trust is released.

Thirdly, it is important to do something about the ongoing judgments and expectations which cause separation in today's relationships because of our inability to trust. These judgments and the whole structure of thinking and expectation behind them must be brought to death on the cross.

Inability to trust God

The third and most devastating consequence of broken trust is the inability to trust God. We can only know God to the degree that we are prepared to trust Him. Trust is an essential element for a growing relationship with our heavenly Father.

The picture of two hands on a Father's Day card was very simple. The large hand of the father reached down to take the small hand of the child. The very simple words inside the card were an affirmation that the child trusted the father. To trust our heavenly Father is simply to put our hand into His strong hand, trusting Him with every step of our journey. Can you begin to do that – to put your hand in His?

God expects us to trust Him

God expects us to trust Him, just as He expects us to love Him, to honor Him and to obey Him. In Luke 15:11–32 there are two prodigals. The younger son dishonored and disobeyed his father, but he came to his senses. When he returned to his father he was welcomed, forgiven, accepted, and restored.

The father didn't say to himself, "This son of mine has a bad track record. I must keep an eye on him. He could go off the rails again." No! The father received him as his son, and amazingly he even trusted him. The shoes and the ring were a symbol that he was received back as a trusted son, and not as a slave.

God trusts us

The Bible clearly teaches that we are saved by grace. This means we are welcomed unreservedly and undeservedly into the family of God on the merits of what Christ did on the cross. Whatever our past, God does not hold it against us. When God forgives, like the father of the prodigal, He trusts us as though we had never sinned. He starts with a new creation, and takes the risk of trusting this newcomer into His family. Our heavenly Father wants His children to know the happiness that comes from living in a mutually trusting relationship. We can never be the loser. God cannot fail. He is utterly trustworthy. Even though He knows our frailties, He still chooses to trust us and give us freedom to make choices. This is called amazing grace.

The other prodigal

The elder son was also a prodigal son. Though he never left his father's house, he never knew his father's heart. Bitterness toward his younger brother, and also toward his father, kept him at a distance. Outwardly he was a perfect son, but inwardly he was a slave with a wall of resentment round his heart which separated him from his father. *"All these years I've been slaving for you and never disobeyed your orders"* (v. 29). He was resentful and grudging, resenting his father's gracious dealings with his younger brother.

The father's reply was simple: *"My son, you are always with me, and everything I have is yours"* (v. 31). Both sons were equally valued and equally loved. In the father's heart there was a unique place for each of them. One son took that place. He was embraced by his father and welcomed home. The other son was consumed by bitterness. He suffered from a sense of injustice. He considered his father unfair – he did not trust his judgment. Consequently, he forfeited the reality of living in an intimate relationship of trust with his father. Trust and intimacy cannot be separated. Without trust there will not be intimacy.

Father God is the father with the longing heart. His children are highly valued and protected by Him. He loves all His children equally, and His love bank never runs dry.

The words of Zephaniah 3:17 were spoken to Israel long ago. They speak to many of God's children today of His heart for them.

> *The LORD your God is with you, he is mighty to save. He will take great delight in you, he will quiet you with his love, he will rejoice over you with singing.*

These words are a picture of the Father heart of God. As a father, He takes great delight in His children. When a child is troubled, He brings quietness to the inner turmoil. Imagine the safety of His arms of love as He rejoices over you with singing. He is the trustworthy Father. Ask Him to reveal His Father heart to you.

Great is Your faithfulness, O God my Father

Healing for the damage of broken trust, and the underlying insecurity, will only be found in God our Father. Where does your place of security in God come from? It comes from the knowledge that He is faithful. *"Your love, O LORD, reaches to the heavens, your faithfulness to the skies"* (Psalm 36:5). We cannot separate the love of God from the faithfulness of God. Both are immeasurable. God cannot fail.

Stepping Stone 8

Has your trust been broken in the past? If so, are there people you need to forgive? If you find it hard to trust God, take hold of a promise from His Word and make it your own, trusting your heavenly Father to fulfill it. Ask Him now to give you one.

CHAPTER 9

To Know This Love That Surpasses Knowledge

When I became a Christian, I was in a church where it was regularly said, "Love is not a feeling. It is a fact." Of course in many ways love is a fact, and we show our love through actions and words; our love for God and for others is shown in how we choose to behave toward them. But love is also an emotion, and what each of us needs more than anything else is a revelation of the love of God for us personally. How does this happen? Revelation of this personal love doesn't come to our heads – it comes to our human spirits, and it touches us in our deepest emotions.

The revelation of God's love comes as a gift from the Holy Spirit. It may happen that we are reading the Bible, and suddenly a truth comes alive to us personally. This is called a *rhema* word, one that we know has been spoken to the deepest place of our heart, and we are changed by it. Again, in healing prayer the personal revelation of God's love can come through a word of knowledge, through a picture or even through a gentle touch. To receive this revelation of the love of God there must, of course, be a hunger for it. It may mean we have to let go of a lesser love to receive the greatest love.

Our human hearts crave for love. It is how God made us. We were born with the need to be loved unconditionally. We were born with a need for love, which God intended would be met through godly parenting. When our need for love has not been met in our early years, we will grow into adulthood craving for love. As a result, we will fail to become people who give love without wanting anything in return, and we will seek to meet our craving for love in ungodly ways.

As adults, what we need now is not human love. We need to feel loved by God. John 3:16 is one of the best-known verses in the Bible. It brought me to Christ when, by divine revelation, I knew that God loved me. Jesus died for the world, and that meant He died for me personally.

> *For God so loved the world that he gave his one and only Son, that whoever believes in him shall not perish but have eternal life.*

I simply substituted my name in the place of *the world*, and knew without a shadow of doubt that I was loved by Jesus, and treasured as a child of the Father. Why not do that with your name right now?

God's love is amazing love. There is nothing you can do to make Him love you more or less. The light of His love for you can never be extinguished. Your failures and messes can't stop Him loving you. His love doesn't depend on your pleasing Him. Amazing!

So does that mean we can sin, and there will be no consequences? No, He does ask us to love Him in return. One-sided love doesn't work! When we love God, we will want to please Him, and follow His ways.

What does love mean?

Can anyone truly define love? There are thousands of definitions, but a person who has never experienced love will be unable to understand it even if they know these definitions. When a person falls in love they are not interested in definitions. The feeling of love comes into every part of their being – they know what love is. Love can only be understood by the experience of it, both God's love and human love.

The four loves

There are, of course, languages of love and love can mean different things to different people. C.S. Lewis in his book, *The Four Loves,*[1] puts love into four categories, using four Greek words:

1. *Storge* (pronounced store-jay): *Storge* love is family love. It is this love which bonds a child to its parents. It is a love of affection, empathy, tenderness, and nurture. This love binds a child to its mother and father as love is expressed in different ways. Every child needs a mother and a father to impart *storge* love from the time of conception right through the teenage years. This love is expressed through

a. Affectionate touch, which conveys to the baby or small child that he or she is important, they belong and have value. The comfort of affectionate touch is something that children of non-tactile parents are deprived of.

b. Eye contact is another way of expressing *storge* love. As the child looks into the eyes of the mother or father, they drink in love.

c. Tone of voice is an expression of love. Gentle caressing words draw something from deep within the child as he or she responds audibly, even before they can understand language.

d. Spirit to spirit communication is a means of bonding parent to child. Something of the depth of love in the mother or father's heart is communicated as the child is nestled in their arms. The human spirit is being nurtured, and a secure foundation is being laid for the child to build his or her life upon.

---

1. C.S. Lewis, *The Four Loves* (London: Collins Fontana Books, 1973).

2. *Phileo*: This is the love on which friendships are based. It is a pure mutual love between kindred spirits, often based on mutual interests. It is possible to have many people whom we call friends, but *phileo* love is grown out of the mutual sharing of hearts where there is a basis of trust.

3. *Eros*: This is the state of being in love. *Eros* love includes sexual love, but it is not sex. A person can have sex without love, and a person can experience *eros* love without the sexual act.

4. *Agape*: *Agape* is the word used in the New Testament to describe God's love. It is a word that expresses the essential nature of God. Agape love is actively interested in the true welfare of others. Love can only be known by the actions it prompts, and God's love in all its fullness is expressed in the gift of His Son. *Agape* love is the love between Christians in whose heart the love of God has been placed by the Holy Spirit.

Storge love is foundational love. It lays a firm foundation for a life to be built upon. If this foundation is not laid in early years, it is often difficult for a person to make sense of the other three loves. *Phileo* love becomes distorted. Friendships often don't work because they are based on need instead of mutual sharing. *Eros* love becomes defiled. Ungodly sexual experiences replace the state of being in love, in an effort to fill the emptiness created by lack of *storge* love. Only *agape* love – God's pure, unselfish, tender love – can satisfy the longings of the heart aching for love.

Helen's story

Helen came from the other side of the world to Ellel Grange for one of our weekend courses. Having been to churches and healing centers in different parts of the world for help, she was in despair. For as long back as she could remember, she had known deep anxiety. She was overtaken with anxiety intermittently during the day, and she would awake at night with the same distressed feeling, often without an obvious reason.

The teaching on *storge* love made sense to Helen. When she was born her mother suffered from post-natal depression, and was unable to bond to or nurture her child. She was emotionally separated and, for short periods of time, physically separated. Her father was distant, and had little input into Helen's life. She had lived her life trying to gain approval and acceptance. Seeking love, Helen had been involved in several sexual relationships.

For Helen it was the beginning of a healing process. She knew she had met Jesus afresh, and her image of a severe distant God was replaced with that of a Father whose love is freely given.

The love void in a human heart cannot be filled with human love. Only God Himself can restore and heal the wounds of neglect. As a person journeys in relationship with God, inner emptiness is gradually and increasingly filled with His divine presence. Our Father in heaven never fails to hear the deep heart cries of His children. He forever waits for His child to turn to Him, and find the comfort that He alone can give.

What the Bible says about love

Love in the Bible is always "giving love." Love in the Bible usually means sacrifice, which is one person freely giving for another person, without thought of reward. That is how God is.

> *This is how God showed his love among us: He sent his one and only Son into the world that we might live through him. This is love: not that we loved God, but that he loved us and sent his Son as an atoning sacrifice for our sins.*
>
> (1 John 4:9–10)

The cross speaks loudly. It simply says, "This is what I mean when I say I love you." The death of Jesus is the ultimate expression of God's love.

What does God mean when He says, "I love you"?

God never ceases to give Himself for others. In the words of A.W. Tozer:

> *An infinite God can give all of Himself to each of His children. He does not distribute Himself that each may have a part, but to each one He gives all of Himself, as fully as if there were no others. God's love is self-giving. He gives for the benefit of others. This shows that it is God's nature to give Himself in order to bring about blessing for the good of others.*[2]

This love is equal for all of God's children. He is Father to us all, and in the capacity of Father He freely gives of Himself. Before we can receive this love which is freely available, we must have a foundation to build on. Many people can see God loves other people, but not them. The foundation upon which we must build is the truth, and that truth is "God loves me." However, many of us believe that God only loves us if we deserve it, if we try to please Him.

You don't have to be good enough

Many of God's children don't feel good enough. They try to make themselves better. The good news is you don't have to be good enough. The devil loves self-improvement programs. He

---

2. A.W. Tozer, *Man: The Dwelling Place of God* (Milton Keynes: Authentic, 2008).

gets on the bandwagon to reinforce what you already think – you're not good enough. If you were good enough, Jesus would never have had to die on the cross. He didn't come to save good people. He came to save sinners. God's love doesn't depend on our goodness. It depends on His grace and mercy to the undeserving. And that includes us all.

God's love is freely given. It is not a controlling love. It can only be experienced in intimate relationship with Him. The fact that we are called *children of God* is evidence that God has lavished His love upon us. We are children of God, and the day is coming when this wonderful truth will become an even greater reality (1 John 3:1–2).

God's love is giving. His supreme gift is the gift of His Son. Someone with such an overflowing heart of love will certainly give us everything we need to fulfill what He has already begun in our lives. There is nothing for our good and for His glory that He withholds.

Julie and Tom had one child, a son called John. In his early twenties, John's one desire was to serve God in foreign mission. Eventually the door was open for him to go with a small team to a deprived part of the world. Three months later, Julie and Tom received a phone call in the middle of the night to say that their only son had suddenly died. They were shocked, as were many others who knew and loved John.

Heartbreak is a reality. Grief and mourning are real life experiences. This experience didn't comfortably fit with the "giving" love of God. God had taken away. Yet at the funeral of their son, Julie and Tom were able to say, "The Lord gave and the Lord has taken away. Blessed be the name of the Lord."

God's love is unshakeable. It is unshakeable because it doesn't depend on anything outside of itself. Whatever may afflict us – troubles, hardships, tragedies, deprivation, sadness, and even our sinfulness – cannot shake the love of God for us. Because He is love He cannot fail to love.

God's love is personal. In love He has planned what is best for each of His children. His plans are for good, and not for harm. Plans to bring hope and a worthwhile future (Jeremiah 29:11).

Just before Jesus went to the cross the disciples were sorrowful. Jesus said to them, "*... the Father himself loves you because you have loved me and have believed that I came from God*" (John 16:27). The disciples received from the lips of Jesus an assurance of the Father's personal love for each one of them – "*the Father himself loves you ...*" Dark times were ahead for those first disciples, and yet they would never be outside of the personal love of the Father Jesus had revealed to them.

A little later, as Jesus prayed for all believers He prayed, "*May they be brought to complete unity to let the world know that you sent me and have loved them even as you have loved me*" (John 17:23). Jesus seems to be saying that the Father's children are loved with the same love as He loves His one and only Son. The love the Father has for Jesus is the same for every one of us, His undeserving children. It is amazing love. The prayer of Jesus was that this deeply personal love the Father has for every one of His children would unite them. All equally loved, all living in the experience of that love, they would be a witness to the world of God's gift of Jesus.

God's love is disciplining. God's discipline is not punishment. Discipline is evidence that we are children of God, for in disciplining us He is treating us as His own children (see Hebrews 12:7).

Discipline is something that few of us like, but true parental love involves discipline. Children brought up with godly discipline will grow up to respect their parents. If this is the case,

> *How much more should we submit to the Father of our spirits and live! Our fathers disciplined us for a little while as they thought best; but God disciplines us for our good, that we may share in his holiness.*
>
> (Hebrews 12:9–10)

God disciplines His children in love, not in anger. His motive for doing so is always for our good, and to make us more like Jesus, for that is what it means to be holy. Discipline deals with our old sinful nature. Through discipline God is refining us.

God's love is restoring. To restore something is to bring it back to its original state, to bring it back to its former condition. David was a shepherd. In his job as a shepherd he must have dealt with many damaged and wounded sheep in need of restoration. But when he wrote Psalm 23 he wrote as a sheep, not a shepherd, and said of the Great Shepherd, *"he restores my soul" (v. 3).*

If sheep are not properly cared for, and are allowed to wander unattended, they become sick or helpless. On one occasion when we were out walking, my husband and I came across a sheep lying on its back, with its legs in the air. It was stuck. It could not help itself. We took the farmer to the place where the sheep lay, and he immediately turned it over onto its legs. The sheep was so weak it stumbled and staggered and then collapsed, so the farmer then held it between his legs until the sheep had enough strength to walk again.

The farmer explained that a sheep in this position was called a **cast sheep**. In that position it was unable to help itself, and if it was left for too long it would die. It could not restore itself. We are sometimes like the cast sheep. Events and experiences of our lives have left us unable to help ourselves, but God does not abandon us. His restoring love and power is for our healing.

If sheep roam about too long on soft, marshy, dirty land they can develop **footrot**. This is a debilitating problem that affects their ability to find food, and if they are left for too long in this condition they can die. The shepherd has to use a knife to trim off parts of the hoof which are damaged. It is a painful process for the sheep, but it is necessary to bring health and restoration.

In the same way, the journey of restoration in our lives can be painful. To own your condition and the causes of deep wounds is not easy. God's restoring love is also healing love. The One who restores us is *Jehovah-Rapha* – the Lord who heals.

What are the blockages to experiencing the love of God?

None of us has been perfectly loved, but some have been more perfectly loved than others. Our experiences of past human love can stand between us and a living experience of God's personal, fatherly love for us. Father experiences can act as a lens through which you see Father God. These blockages don't simply disappear. It is important to own the past as it really was, in order to move some of the blockages between you and the heart of God.

Ellen's story

Ellen had been on the road to healing for several years, and yet she seemed stuck. When I met her, she had come to the point of being willing to face any pain in her life that was blocking her relationship with God. Ellen's head and heart told different stories. She was extremely loyal to her parents. She had convinced herself that her childhood was very happy, and her father was as near to perfect as a father could be. She couldn't recall any unhappy times. Her emotional state as an adult and her relationship with God seemed to tell a different story.

Ellen had lived in denial all her life, and it was a painful process for her to begin to own some of the issues that had caused deep wounds in her heart. These wounds were father wounds, and they had distorted her understanding of Father God. Healing her father wounds was a process – a distressing process – because she had to come from unreality into reality.

Ellen's father had not been angry or abusive, but he had been emotionally absent, and withdrew into moods of long silence, which in the core of her being Ellen believed were her fault. Consequently, when things went wrong in adult life she felt it was always her fault. She longed to know God as an intimate Father, and yet He seemed distant and could not help her.

Ellen's father had done many good things for her – she loved him and believed that he loved her. Owning the truth as it was didn't diminish Ellen's love for her father. She knew that to the extent he was able, he loved her. However, owning the truth about him was the stepping stone to the Father heart of God.

Past experiences can distort our view of God's love

From an early age, many people have had conditions put on receiving love. They have developed an internal core belief that love has to be earned by being good, doing well, pleasing people, obeying rules, and many more things. A person who has not lived in the experience of unconditional love finds it hard to understand what true love really is. Consequently they have a distorted understanding of real love.

Love is dangerous or painful

When our experience of childhood and adult relationships has not been good, the false belief that love is painful and dangerous is reinforced. Repeated failure in relationships sows the seeds of the belief "I am not worthy of love." We then transfer this to God's love, forgetting that God's love is freely given as a gift.

The belief that love is dangerous or painful can come from a variety of sources. Controlling or demanding relationships open doorways to fear and insecurity in the person on whom the demands are made. Control can be by actions, words, looks or attitudes. Any kind of abuse is controlling, whether the abuse is physical, emotional, sexual or spiritual. Abuse takes away a person's free will, and leaves a state of confusion. A person who has been controlled in childhood develops a deep need to control in later relationships.

Once we were on holiday in the Canadian Rockies, and we did a most incredible walk under the leadership of a guide called Michelle. Michelle had a history of broken relationships and was deeply hurting on the inside. She came to a point where she had had enough, and decided she would get a dog to try to fill the void in her life. A colleague persuaded Michelle that a cat would be a better option because cats could be controlled more easily, and so she got a cat.

Michelle told me the most remarkable stories about the cat. She had trained it to do exactly as she wanted, and she took it with her on long walks through the mountains. When I said that her escapades with the cat would make interesting reading, she told me she was writing a book for children to show them that without love and trust, relationships do not stand a chance.

Control is incompatible with love

Michelle, like many people, had concluded that love was painful. Our conversation revealed that she needed to control relationships, and that seemed to be the reason for the many breakdowns.

Though God is in control of all that He has made, He does not control people. He always gives them the choice to love and obey Him, or to disobey Him. Wounded people often try to control God in that they think He should do what they ask Him to do. When He doesn't, there is often a question raised about God's love.

Our culture has distorted the meaning of love. A belief that "love takes away control of your life" usually comes from the negative experiences of childhood which have distorted the true meaning of intimacy. Fear of intimacy is fear of love. Our society distorts the meaning of love in different ways. Two main ways are:

A. LOVE IS PRIMARILY SEXUAL

In our culture, people's idea of love tends to be primarily sexual. The connotations behind the word "relationship" are usually sexual. Relationship addiction is real. Many people cannot live without being in a sexual relationship. They are looking for love, but the empty love hole in their heart cannot be filled through multiple sexual relationships. Only the love of God can fill it. Empty father-holes are a breeding ground for sexual sin as the hungry person seeks to fill their inner emptiness.

B. LOVE DOESN'T LAST

In a world where the traditional family has almost died out, where divorce is easily available, where "free love" abounds, and the rights of children are being eroded, the message we receive is that love doesn't last.

Jane's father left home when she was a few weeks old, and he had little to do with her throughout childhood. Her mother brought home different partners who stayed for a time then disappeared. She grew up without a model of permanent relationships, and could not believe that her heavenly Father's love was an enduring and unending love.

In Jane's life were issues of rejection, abandonment, loneliness, injustice, and unfairness. These issues had to be owned and faced for the healing power of the cross to touch deep into her heart. During prayer times for the neglect in her childhood, Father God revealed Himself to Jane through words and pictures that touched her spirit with healing love.

Why do I find it hard to enter fully into the Father's love?

People often feel frustrated. They want to know God more intimately, and to experience His love for them personally. To receive love is to receive a person. It is to meet a person, to love that person, and to know yourself loved by that person. In the Father heart of God there is abounding, inexhaustible love. The Father's heart is a longing heart, and all His children are special and chosen. God is perfect, and His love is perfect, so if I cannot fully enter into His love, the problem must lie with me.

There can be blockages in us that keep us from Father love. We looked at some earlier, and we will look at some more in the following chapters. Two of the main blockages are:

1. Strongholds in the mind

The apostle Paul says that strongholds are built in our minds, and they contain patterns of wrong thinking (2 Corinthians 10:5). A stronghold is a fortified area in our mind that forces us to think in a certain direction. When we repeatedly and consistently act and think in wrong ways, strongholds develop in our minds. Negative thoughts and feelings of hopelessness flourish in a spiritual stronghold, fulfilling the enemy's purpose to keep us back from truly knowing God.

Strongholds grow out of shattered dreams. We start thinking in patterns based on untrue assumptions. Strongholds grow from painful experiences and broken trust. They are built by the devil; he is a thief and a robber.

> *He was a murderer from the beginning, not holding to the truth, for there is no truth in him. When he lies, he speaks his native language, for he is a liar and the father of lies.*
>
> (John 8:44)

The father of lies and hatred opposes the Father of truth and love.

2. Wounds of the heart

Wounds of the heart usually go a long way back in our history. From these wounds we develop a distorted picture of God. Even in mature Christians there can be something that lingers underneath the surface that seems to block intimacy with God, trust in God, and the experience of knowing they are absolutely safe, secure, and fear-free in the knowledge of the Father's love.

Something in the heart has given a wrong view of God as He really is. The deepest of these wounds are parental wounds. From birth every child needs to be physically and emotionally attached to their parents, especially their mother. Attachment takes place when a child is nurtured and bonded in the way God intended through words, touch, looks, and time. This gives the child the message that they belong and they are safe, and the message is conveyed to the human spirit of the child. When this process is missing, the message picked up is one of detachment accompanied by feelings of insecurity, fear, and anxiety.

Joseph's story

Joseph's story can be summed up in the word "detachment." His mother and father ran a family business, and unfortunately the process of bonding and nurture failed to take place. Joseph's mother already had three older children so he was left to cry a lot as a baby, and he was left to his own devices as a pre-school toddler. His father was always exhausted when he came home from work. As a small boy, Joseph could remember running to sit on his father's knee. Sometimes he was accepted, and other times he was rejected. His father's moods were unpredictable.

Joseph was spiritually mature. He held a responsible position in Christian ministry. He loved God, and had experiences of closeness with God. Deep inside, however, he was often troubled, fearful, and anxious. In the deepest place of his heart he felt not quite acceptable to God, and not quite sure of His unconditional love. This, accompanied by a lingering sense of shame and exhaustion from work overload, led Joseph to seek ministry because he knew something was not quite right.

In prayer ministry, the Holy Spirit dealt with the things that Joseph could remember, but also with the things too deeply hidden in the heart for him to recall. As the wounds were healed, the strongholds were broken down, and that missing thing of utter peace and joy in God was restored to Joseph as he was healed through the wounds of Jesus who died for our salvation. Joseph was brought to a place of wholeness where he no longer lived out of diseased childhood emotions, but from an assurance of his worth and value as a child of God.

Dealing with emotional pain

Unless we deal with our emotional pain from the past, it will keep creeping into the present, and sometimes overwhelm us when it comes from deep wounds. Our pain needs to be exchanged for God's comfort. Adult pain is often rooted in the lack of parental comfort in childhood.

People are frequently told, "Take your pain to the cross." The reply usually goes something like, "That is what I want to do, but I don't know how." To take our pain to the cross can seem an easy thing to say. However, each of us must first own our pain. It is part of our history, part of us, and what we have become. Jesus didn't die to negate our pain. Jesus died to heal our wounds. For our wounds to be healed we need to identify with our pain, to accept it happened, hold it, and allow Jesus to link us with any memories we have disowned.

It is tempting when pain rises to the surface to begin to push it down again. We cannot heal ourselves or get our act together. No earthly person can heal our pain. That would deny what Jesus had to do for us on the cross. The healing of our deepest pain is rooted in the unconditional love God has for us, love that we see on the cross.

God doesn't will or cause our pain. Neither does He make it suddenly disappear. He heals our wounds, and then our pain is released, and we are embraced by His divine love.

Stepping Stone 9

Ask yourself if there are strongholds in your mind or wounds in your heart that keep you from living in the perfect love of God in which there is no fear. Are you willing to face reality, and receive the healing love of God for yourself?

CHAPTER 10

The Father Heart of God in Suffering

The issue of suffering is probably the most challenging one to the Christian faith. We are constantly confronted by suffering, and not a single person goes through life untouched. The Bible gives a good deal of attention to suffering. An example is the Psalms, which could be called the prayers of the Old Testament. In them we find cries of "Why?" that arise out of doubt, disappointment, pain, and confusion.

The New Testament also has a lot to say about suffering. In the New Testament, however, we do not find the same questions that we find in the Old Testament, such as, "Does God care?" "Has He forgotten me?" and "Why has this come upon me?"

The New Testament speaks about joy, confidence, and hope even in the midst of suffering. Even the greatest suffering cannot overwhelm the heart of the believer. Something has happened to make the difference. God has made Himself known in the person of Jesus Christ. He has revealed His Father heart.

What is suffering?

Suffering is different for each of us but it is usually linked with a sense of loss, injustice, or deprivation of what is rightfully ours.

Suffering is a demonic intrusion into the world. God created humankind to have an uninterrupted and unbroken relationship with Himself. Jesus confronted suffering, and the demonic powers behind it. When He rebuked the spirit of infirmity in the woman who had been bound by Satan for eighteen years, Jesus spoke the words, *"Woman, you are set free from your infirmity"* (Luke 13:12).

Love and free will

Each of us was created for a loving relationship with God and with other humans. Love cannot exist where there is no freedom to choose. Free will was a gift given to us at creation. Sin and suffering came into the world when free will was misused in an act of disobedience to God.

God gave the gift of free will out of love for those He created. Love is not love if it is forced. In true love there is always choice and freedom. Because God loves us He gives us a choice. To love Him in return, and demonstrate our love by obedience, or not to love Him and go our own way. From the beginning men and women have chosen to go their own way, make wrong choices and disobey God. Disobedience to God is sin, and the result is suffering. This does not mean, of course, that all suffering is due to individual sin, or that suffering is God's way of punishing someone for his or her sin.

Suffering is part of being human

Suffering is not what God planned. Before the Fall there was no pain, suffering or death. Suffering is a major part of death, and the Bible clearly says that death came through sin.

> *... just as sin entered the world through one man, and death through sin, and in this way death came to all men, because all sinned ...*
>
> (Romans 5:12)

Because sin came into the world, death and suffering have become the legacy of every human being born into the world.

Suffering as a consequence of our own sin

Our own sin brings suffering. If we break God's law, we inevitably reap the consequences. The law of sowing and reaping comes into effect.

> *Do not be deceived: God cannot be mocked. People reap what they sow.*
> (Galatians 6:7 TNIV)

If a person abuses drugs or alcohol or uses pornography, they will become addicted, causing suffering to themselves and to those related to them. Similarly selfishness, anger, abuse, lust, and pride often lead to broken relationships, which cause deep suffering. Many of us know what it is to suffer as a consequence of our own sin.

Suffering as a consequence of the sin of others

Secondly, the sin of others causes suffering. Sin committed against us may be on a personal, community, national or global level. Almost daily we hear news of suffering on a global scale. Wars, disasters, famine, starvation, and widespread deprivation are all too common.

Such tragedies bring suffering to countless lives on local and national levels. A team from Ellel Ministries are in Rwanda as I write, ministering to some of the countless people who experienced man's inhumanity to man during the genocide.

Suffering is also caused by the sin of others on an individual level. Childhood neglect and deprivation resulting in lifelong emotional turmoil, abuse, adultery, poverty, bullying, injustice, lying, stealing, murder, violence, and much more can cause untold individual suffering.

Suffering is never good in itself

The Bible acknowledges that pain and grief are part of being human in a fallen world, whether or not a person is a Christian. We would all like to escape suffering, but God can and does use it for good. In his book, *The Problem of Pain*, C.S. Lewis wrote that suffering was the instrument of God to rouse a world that was deaf.[1] God uses suffering even though He does not cause it. He uses it to help us to realize that there is more to life than material things. In our suffering, our loving Father draws us to consider His love, draws us to find comfort in Himself, and causes us to turn to Him.

Suffering develops character

The Bible teaches that God uses suffering to develop character.

> *... suffering produces perseverance, perseverance, character; and character, hope.*
>
> (Romans 5:3-4)

Character is different to reputation. Reputation is what others think we are. Character is what we are before God. God can use suffering to develop our character, so that the life of Jesus grows within us.

1. C.S. Lewis, *The Problem of Pain* (New York: HarperOne, 2001).

Suffering tests faith

Suffering is one of the themes in Peter's letters. The New Testament believers suffered for their faith, and Peter wrote to encourage them.

> *... for a little while you may have had to suffer grief in all kinds of trials. These have come so that your faith – of greater worth than gold, which perishes even though refined by fire – may be proved genuine ...*
>
> (1 Peter 1:6–7)

Suffering is certainly a test of faith. Genuine faith stands the test and is refined in suffering. The picture here is of a metalworker refining gold, heating the furnace to such a high temperature that all the impurities in the metal rise to the surface, and can be skimmed off. Through suffering God tests our faith, but he also refines us in the refiner's fire to bring out something good.

God works suffering for our good

In all His dealings with His children, God desires their good, never harm. Nothing can enter our lives outside of His permissive will. Ultimately, He is in control. If we trust Him, despite loss, sorrow, and sadness for a time, He will bring the end result to something good.

> *And we know that in all things God works for the good of those who love him, who have been called according to his purpose.*
>
> (Romans 8:28)

It is God who is working in times of suffering. He is working for our good, although at the time the end is hidden from us. In our darkest hour He asks us to trust Him. He is a good Father, and despite our sorrow and sadness, He has our good at heart.

Lisa Goertz was a Jewish lady who lost most of her family in the Nazi holocaust, including her mother, husband, brother, son, and daughter. At one point, when sixteen members of her family had disappeared, she decided to end it all. In her book, *I Stepped into Freedom*, she tells what happened:

> *I walked out into the night, feeble with hunger, half crazy with fear and fatigue, and made my way down to the river Neisse. In a few hours all would be over, I told myself. What a relief! And there it happened. Across the dark river I saw the cross and Jesus Christ on it. His face was not the face of a victor; it was the face of a fellow-sufferer, full of love and understanding and compassion. We gazed at each other, both of us Jews, and then the vision disappeared.*[2]

For Lisa this was the beginning of the road that led to faith and personal healing. God used suffering that was almost beyond human endurance to give her an understanding of His heart of compassion shown in the death of Jesus, and to transform her suffering.

God is not indifferent to suffering

On 21 October 1966, 144 people, 116 of them children, were killed in what became known as the Aberfan Disaster in South Wales. Coal waste from the mountain above the village of Aberfan rushed down the mountain, first destroying a cottage, and then engulfing the school and some houses in the village. Half the children in the school and five of their teachers were among the dead.

The cause was an underground spring, and two days of

2. Lisa Goertz, *I Stepped into Freedom* (Cambridge: Lutterworth Press, 1960).

heavy rain that loosened the coal waste on the mountain. The Aberfan Disaster was not a natural one. The enquiry ruled that negligence on the part of the Coal Board was responsible.

As parents were searching for their children, a lady demanded angrily of a local clergyman, "Where is your God now?" He replied, "Underneath the rubble with the children." Our God is not indifferent to suffering. He suffers with those who suffer.

We may feel angry with God at times. Life may seem unfair or unjust. The One whom Jesus revealed to us as Father understands how we are made. He can truly enter into our heartbreak. On the cross His heart was broken too.

Why do I suffer so much pain?

Often the question is asked, "Why do I suffer so much pain?" Debilitating physical pain is hard to bear. Undiagnosable physical pain is sometimes tied deep into emotional pain, and remains until the inner wounding is healed.

Tim's story

On his first visit to Ellel Grange, Tim did our course "Restoring the Human Spirit." During the teaching he spent a considerable time in tears, not fully understanding what was happening. He had been involved in missionary work for several years, had experienced considerable disappointment, and was quite angry toward God.

Tim's relationship with his father had been difficult, lacking acceptance and affirmation. Part way through the course, Tim faced the pain and wounding in his heart, and forgave his father as the Holy Spirit brought to him hidden memories. He received a wonderful revelation of his heavenly Father, and was overwhelmed by His love and acceptance.

Several years prior to the course, Tim had been involved in a horrific road accident following which he needed several operations to different parts of his body. His final state was that he couldn't bend his knees; getting up and down stairs was difficult, to say nothing of the pain. He walked with the aid of a walking stick.

Tim had been traumatized by the accident, and his inner pain needed to be healed by God. After receiving prayer, Tim was found running up and down the stairs, walking stick in the rubbish bin, shouting, "I'm healed, I'm healed!" His physical pain had gone, and his body was healed. He had received prayer for inner healing without any mention of his physical needs.

Some people are cut off from their emotions, whilst others have an overflow of inappropriate emotions. They feel pain and cannot always identify why. They have hidden memories of experiences that have been too painful to handle at the time it happened. Inner pain doesn't simply go away. It remains until its roots are exposed and healed.

God, it's not fair

During times of suffering, life can seem unfair. At such times it is tempting to think that God is neither fair nor just. And yet justice is one of His attributes. In both the Old and New Testaments, the word used for righteousness can also be translated as justice. God's righteousness means that He always does what is right. Speaking of God, Moses says, "*… all his ways are just. A faithful God who does no wrong, upright and just is he*" (Deuteronomy 32:4). God's justice cannot be separated from His faithfulness. He is a faithful God who does no wrong. God's justice cannot be separated from His mercy and His forgiveness:

> *The Lord our God is merciful and forgiving, even though we have rebelled against him.*
>
> (Daniel 9:9)

The human reaction to injustice is often revenge. We want others to suffer as we have suffered to make us feel better. Of course it doesn't work like that. Yet anger about injustice is not wrong. Injustice is unfairness, and it is right to feel angry about injustice and unfairness. The problem is in how that anger is expressed. When it is expressed in the wrong way, it brings even more suffering.

When we are suffering unjustly, for us to come to peace from turmoil, we will need to come to that place where we realize that what we have in God is greater than any loss or injustice. We have a God who heals the broken-hearted. We have a God who has mercy on those who suffer. We have a God who comforts us in our troubles. As a father comforts his child, so the One who is perfect in His fathering promises to comfort us in our suffering with His own divine presence. The psalmist could say,

> *My comfort in my suffering is this: Your promise preserves my life.*
>
> (Psalm 119:50)

People just like us

The Bible is a book about suffering. It acknowledges that suffering is part of human life, even for those who love God. The Old Testament describes many situations where there is suffering, including the same kinds of things that cause suffering in the world today.

As we read the Old Testament, we read of appalling suffering both on a national and individual level. Yet, as we see God at work in His world, we can never doubt that He is a God who suffers with those who suffer. However terrible the circumstances, God's heart is toward His people and He works for their good. God redeems our losses with His own promise of comfort and hope.

Here are some examples of suffering endured by those people of old, and also by us.

Jealousy

Joseph was Jacob's favorite son, and his brothers were jealous. Their jealousy turned to such hatred that they were ready to kill him.

> *"Here comes that dreamer!" they said to each other. "Come now, let's kill him and throw him into one of these cisterns and say that a ferocious animal devoured him."*
>
> (Genesis 37:19–20)

God had plans for Joseph's life, and used his suffering to develop his character so that blessing would flow to others.

To us, jealousy may not seem to be a major sin, but in reality it is one step short of murder. It begins by destroying a person on the inside and then manifests itself in harmful words or actions which cause suffering to those on the receiving end.

Jealousy is one of the most common emotions, but we often fail to see how it can be one of the most dangerous.

False accusation

Job set out on a journey that began with the question, "Why do I suffer?" Three "friends" walked that journey with Job. Sadly, they were false friends who were convinced that Job was suffering because he had sinned. Their harsh judgment only made Job's burden heavier. Their condemnation caused him great confusion, and added to his suffering. In the end, God rewarded Job for his faithfulness in his suffering:

> *The LORD blessed the latter part of Job's life more than the first.*
>
> (Job 42:12)

False accusation hurts and can cause much suffering. Jesus was falsely accused, and it cost Him His life upon the cross. One of the names for Satan is Accuser –

> *… the accuser of our brothers, who accuses them before God day and night, has been hurled down.*
>
> (Revelation 12:10)

Satan is behind false accusation. His intent is to pull down and destroy.

Criticism usually accompanies false accusation. Criticism acts like prayer to the devil, because it has the power to destroy a person's self-worth.

The death of a child

David was devastated when the baby boy that Bathsheba bore to him became ill and was dying. "*David pleaded with God for the child. He fasted and went into his house and spent the nights lying on the ground … he would not eat*" (2 Samuel 12:16–17).

> *… Jacob tore his clothes, put on sackcloth and mourned for his son many days. All his sons and daughters came to comfort him, but he refused to be comforted. "No," he said, "in mourning will I go down to the grave to my son."*
>
> (Genesis 37:34–35)

Whether it's an infant or an adult, the loss of a child brings suffering that at times can be overwhelming. Our second child, a girl, died during the birth process due to negligence by the midwife. She was full term, perfect and beautiful. No provision was made for stillborn children in the 1960s, so this precious child, whom we named Julie, was bundled up in brown paper and taken from our home where she had been born and deposited in an unknown grave.

The church we attended didn't know how to handle sorrow, and they had no explanation for what happened to stillborn children. Was this the end of a longed-for child, or was she in heaven? I was stuck. I seemed unable to move on because I had no hope.

George Beverley Shea of the Billy Graham Association gave a concert in Manchester, where we lived. He sang a song about God having the whole world in His hands, and having that tiny baby in His hands. God spoke hope into my heart. As I listened to the words of the song, I had a picture before me of our merciful heavenly Father holding our tiny baby in His hands. At that moment I knew she was safe, and that I would see her again. My wounded heart began a process of healing. I could now move forward.

The lack of children

The Bible teaches that children are a blessing from the Lord. To be blessed by God meant that you would know joy from enjoying happy circumstances.

A "barren" woman suffered disgrace because infertility was considered to be a shameful mark of divine disfavor. To be a happy woman was to be the mother of many children. To be childless was to suffer humiliation and disgrace.

Hannah longed for a child (1 Samuel 1). As the years went by, her desperation and sorrow grew. She wept and could not eat. In bitterness of soul she prayed. Downcast, in anguish and grief she poured out her soul before the Lord. Her desperation was such that she bargained with God. If He would answer her prayer for a son, she would give him back to God for all the days of his life.

Samuel became the great prophet of Israel used to fulfill the purposes of God. Hannah's prayer was answered in God's way and time. Eventually her suffering was turned to joy.

Childlessness is a cause of suffering today. With very few exceptions, women long to become mothers, and most men desire to become fathers. It is an innate desire, one we were born with, because it is God-given. When God created male and female,

> *God blessed them and said to them, "Be fruitful and increase in number; fill the earth and subdue it."*
>
> (Genesis 1:28)

When you are praying for a person who longs for a child, it is important to listen to God. *"Hope deferred makes the heart sick, but a longing fulfilled is a tree of life"* (Proverbs 13:12). In other words, the more a person is prayed for and the prayer does not bring fruit, the more hopeless the person becomes.

Sometimes there is a physical problem. As we have prayed, sometimes this has been rectified and sometimes it hasn't. Many times there is a spiritual problem resulting from the person's own sin, or from sin on their generational line.

One couple nearing forty years of age desperately desired a child. Medically there was no reason why conception didn't take place. During prayer the man was brought to deep repentance for sexual sin in his past. Though he had confessed this before, he had not seen the seriousness of his sin to God. Within six weeks, their prayers were answered – they were to become parents.

> *If you, then, though you are evil, know how to give good gifts to your children, how much more will your Father in heaven give good gifts to those who ask him!*
>
> (Matthew 7:11)

Our positive experience in praying for many childless people is proof that our heavenly Father desires to give good gifts. It is far wiser to turn toward Him with an open heart, seeking His face and His will, whatever that may be, than to turn away from Him.

Sexual abuse

The Bible doesn't avoid uncomfortable issues. Sexual abuse was not uncommon, but it is something detested by God.

In 2 Samuel 13 we have the story of Amnon, son of David, who raped his half-sister Tamar. Tamar trusted Amnon, and his scheme to get his own way was achieved through trickery, lying, and deception. The effect on Tamar was devastating, and she went into mourning.

Although David was angry at what had happened, it seems he failed to take action. He abdicated his responsibility as a father, leaving Tamar to suffer the consequences without his intervention.

Today, sexual abuse has devastating results. It causes those who have been victims of such sin to blame God and to cry out, "God, if You care about me, why didn't You protect me?" Healing for sexual abuse, and any other abuse, is found in Jesus. He is the One who introduces us to the Father heart of God.

Injustice

Life has been unfair to many people. Many have suffered great injustice, and our human hearts want revenge. God understands – He hates injustice. His requirement from His people was, and still is,

> *To act justly and to love mercy and to walk humbly with your God.*
> (Micah 6:8)

Justice cries out for punishment, not mercy. Feelings of injustice can be overwhelming, especially for people who have been victims of suffering at the mercy of those who gave no mercy.

We can identify with those people in the Bible in so many ways. The danger of death, persecution and hostility, loneliness, abandonment, unfaithfulness, the ingratitude of friends and family, and man's inhumanity to man.

We may find it hard to reconcile suffering with the heart of the One who loves us. He has promised that we shall never be tested or tempted above what we are able to bear, through His grace operating in us. Whatever we have been through, or are going through, He asks us to believe in Him. That is to put our trust actively in Him, believing His promise that He will never leave us or forsake us (Deuteronomy 31:6; Hebrews 13:5).

Dietrich Bonhoeffer was a German theologian who stood beside the innocent, and spoke out against the injustices of Hitler during World War Two. He suffered imprisonment, and was executed at the age of thirty-nine on 9 April 1945. During his time of deep suffering he recorded the following prayer:

> *Father in heaven,*
> *You have shown me many good things,*
> *Let me now accept hard things from You.*
> *You will not place on me more than I can bear;*
> *You make all things serve your children for the best.*[3]

Bonhoeffer trusted himself to his Father in heaven with the firm belief that whatever suffering life holds, this Father has in His heart the best for His children.

---

3. Dietrich Bonhoeffer, *The Cost of Discipleship* (Norwich: SCM Press, 2001).

Stepping Stone 10

Are there painful issues in your life for which you blame God, or feel He has treated you unfairly? Confess this to Him. He longs to comfort you, and heal you, and draw you to Himself.

CHAPTER

11

A Heart to Know God

In Biblical terms, our heart is the center of who we are. From our hearts spring emotions, thoughts, motivations, courage, and action. The heart is the wellspring of life, and in every heart there is a God-shaped hole that only God can fill.

It is with our hearts that we know God, because our heart includes our spirit. With our minds we can understand things about God, but we can only truly know Him with our heart. It is through Jesus and what He has done that mere humans can intimately know God in a way that Old Testament believers never could.

The promise of the new covenant contained the assurance that those who entered in would have a new heart – a heart to **know** God.

> *I will give them a heart to know me, that I am the Lord. They will be my people, and I will be their God, for they will return to me with all their heart.*
>
> (Jeremiah 24:7)

It is possible to know what the Bible teaches, to know all about doctrine, and yet still not to know God. Jack was such a person. Twice every Sunday he preached and taught the Bible – he called it "Bible-based preaching," and yet it didn't seem to change the hearts and lives of the hearers. He admitted that he knew much of what there was to know about God, but didn't know God for himself. He was mercifully brought to the place where he saw that there was something vitally wrong with his heart – something that needed to be radically changed for his knowledge to become experience.

The wounded heart

We can have problems with our hearts. Wounds in our hearts affect how we see God, how we see ourselves, and how we see life. These wounds have usually been there for a long time, and they are full of pain. Wounds in the heart are not simply hurting emotions; they are part of who we are, and who we have become. Who and what we believe we are, we are.

Wounds in our hearts affect our identity – our perception of ourselves. They also affect our destiny – God's purpose for our lives, and how we choose to live that out. Wounds in the heart also affect our perception of God, and who He is. They distort His true character. These wounds are like false glasses through which we view the true Father heart of God.

How we see God liberates Him or blocks Him in His freedom to do things for us and in us. Early life, especially with parents, puts colored glasses on us through which the truth is distorted so that we are unable to grasp it in our hearts. In adult life we may know in our heads the way God is Biblically, but our deep understanding was formed long ago, and will never be rectified by human effort or willpower but only by Jesus, the wounded Healer.

A person with a wounded heart can become more wounded if they are constantly challenged to use their faith and believe the Bible. They desperately want to believe and experience that they are loved as a unique, individual child of God, but the blockage between head and heart just won't go away.

Wounds in the heart can only be healed through Jesus who is

the truth. He alone can unveil the darkness that holds us back from the embrace of our heavenly Father. It is the Lord Jesus Himself who reveals the truth of who we are, and the truth of who the Father is.

A person with a wounded heart develops coping mechanisms to enable them to manage the resulting problems. A common way of coping is by performing well.

The performance heart

The performance heart is driven by the need to do well. Approval in early years has usually been given as a reward for achievement and success. The driven life is a hard life, and it acts as a blockage to receiving the unearned love of God. A relationship based on performance leads a person to feel that God has degrees of love that must be earned. They feel He is a distant God who they cannot be too close to.

A sign of the performing heart is people-pleasing. This is rooted in the wounds of perceived conditional love in childhood. Long ago in childhood, it seemed that if they achieved, worked hard, and got it right, they would be loved. If they got it wrong, failed, didn't work hard or made a mistake, they would be rejected, excluded, and not loved.

People-pleasing comes in different forms, but at its root is the assumption that love has to be earned because it is not freely given. Driven by the pain of childhood wounds, the person constantly strives to please people as a means of gaining their approval.

The same mindset is at work in relation to God. Despite the fact that His love and approval are not earned, people-pleasing tactics are transferred to Him. Such a person finds it much easier to be a servant constantly working, than a child resting in the certain knowledge that they are truly loved.

The hardened heart

The hardened heart is usually a wounded heart. Events of life, disappointments, failures, and sin have hardened the soil of the heart so that good seed does not readily take root. The person whose heart is hardened has usually built defense mechanisms in their life to protect them from further hurt. These defense mechanisms act like walls around the heart, built for protection but they also keep other people at a distance.

The hardened heart is a lonely heart, lacking tenderness and compassion. It has to be recognized for what it is, and the ungodly ways of protecting self acknowledged as sin, which keeps everyone at a distance, including God who desires to draw near. The hardened heart needs softening at the cross to be an abiding place for God's love.

The addicted heart

The addicted heart falls into patterns of behavior which become coping mechanisms for inner pain. Addictions are escape routes from reality. They are sinful and powerful whether hidden or obvious, and act as a blockage to intimacy in relationships, both human and divine.

Addictive behavior takes a person into a world of unreality. Because addictions camouflage pain, the person often refuses to recognize the wounding, and their need for God's healing. Addictions cause delusions and deceptions in many areas of life, and the person learns to live in an unreal world.

A major part of healing is to bring reality into a person's life. God is real, and He relates to real people. For the addicted person to experience the love of God, they must reject the fantasy world as a world where God cannot be found. Self-help is not the answer, but right choices are part of the answer. The addicted heart needs to become a broken heart, a softened heart, where sin is recognized for what it is, with humble acknowledgment that true healing and restoration can only be found in Jesus Christ.

Phoebe's story

Phoebe's story is summed up in her own words, "Journey to the Scars." She had suffered rejection, loneliness, abandonment and loss, and acknowledged that she had been into sin. When I met her she assumed that the issues in her life had been dealt with because they happened a long time ago, and yet she longed for a real meeting with God as her Father.

When Phoebe heard teaching on how our past can hinder our present relationships, she realized that she had been very good at covering her pain and wounds. On the outside she believed she appeared normal, but now started to recognize that she had wounds on top of wounds which she had camouflaged with drugs, alcohol, promiscuity, work, religion, and other things.

Phoebe told me that she realized she had built a life for herself around her hidden wounds. It was an unreal life – a life over which Jesus was not Lord. This revelation of truth to Phoebe, and her willingness to submit to the lordship of Jesus in every area of her life, was the beginning of a new journey. She prayed, "I thank You, Father, for loving me enough to get my attention, and showing me that Your love for me is healing love."

The father-hole in the wounded heart

There are many sons and daughters walking round with a father-shaped hole in their hearts. They have missed things from their father that should have been given. Maybe he responded to them in ungodly ways, was away from home for long periods of time, or simply disappeared from their lives.

Father experiences affect the heart of a child. Many adult children have broken hearts from what they suffered at the hands of their fathers. When sober he could be a good father – caring and likeable – but when drinking, he was angry and destructive.

Lily arrived home late one evening. Her mother was out, and her father was in the house drinking with two of his friends. The look in their eyes made her feel afraid, but before she could escape, one of them grabbed her. Her father looked on while both of his friends sexually assaulted Lily. From that evening, life was never the same. Father wounds were deep in her heart, wounds that no earthly person could heal, wounds that could only be healed through deep forgiveness and a revelation of the love of God shown in the cross.

The emotionally absent father

The emotionally absent father is usually at home, but though he is there in person he is absent – emotionally absent, so that he is unknowable. This father is never available emotionally – he is unavailable to discuss struggles or problems or to give advice. He is not available to help with homework or choosing career options.

The non-affirming father

The non-affirming father does not normally offer praise or acknowledgment. On the rare occasion when he does, it is usually at someone else's prompting. The non-affirming father is sometimes a critical father whose words leave scars on the heart of his child. The child of this father often spends their life looking for his approval and affirmation.

The absent father

This is the father who is not there for his child. It may be through no fault of his own that he is gone from early morning until late at night. When this father is home, he often retreats into the newspaper or turns on the television. This father may be too occupied with his own world to ever enter his child's world.

The angry father

The angry father demands unquestioning obedience, perhaps using intimidation as a weapon. He is often unreasonable, and usually has a short fuse so it doesn't take much for his anger to surface.

The child of this father longs to have a different kind of dad. They long for their dad to change so that they don't have to spend their lives trying to avoid his anger. The wounds from this father are full of deep insecurity – he is so changeable that he cannot be trusted. The angry father fails to comfort and protect. His emotional instability makes it hard for his children to trust him.

What is a father?

What is a father? What is he supposed to be for his child, and what is he supposed to do? Many adult children who come for prayer describe how they wish their fathers had been. Some have created a father image, making him into what they wanted him to be, but this is unreal. In some there is trauma and grief buried in father wounds. In others there is a broken heart – a heart broken by the events of life; a heart broken by father wounds.

God intended our fathers to be windows on the Father heart of God. God made fathers to model Himself, to be honest, trustworthy, compassionate and intimate. Father love should epitomize the love of the Perfect Father. He alone can satisfy the father longings in our wounded hearts. His love was so infinite that He gave His one and only Son who would bind up the broken-hearted.

Healing for the wounded heart

Parental wounds do not simply go away. They must be owned so that the pain can be released. The journey of healing always begins with forgiveness. When we are ministering to those with wounded hearts, we know we cannot hurry the process. The Holy Spirit knows where to touch a person when they are willing to face reality. Forgiveness is never cheap, but true forgiveness is life-changing. During prayer for the healing of parental wounds, men and women often weep like little children as by the grace of God they forgive the unforgivable.

Father God intervenes. We are not always aware of His presence, but He is always there. He was there at the beginning of your life, in your infancy and childhood, in your teenage years and young adult life. He is here in the present watching over you, His beloved child. He knows all that has happened.

He binds up even the broken-hearted. His heart for His children is revealed through Jesus. He wants to father His children in true fatherhood, because He wants each of us to share in His beautiful holiness.

Our heavenly Father loves us as we are – in our pain, immaturity, neediness, and desperation. He loves us too much to leave us where we are. So great is His love that He prepared the way to redeem what was lost, restore what was broken, and heal that which has been wounded.

He heals the orphan heart

On one occasion when I was teaching on the Father heart of God at Ellel Grange, two men began weeping profusely. One was at the front of the room and the other at the back, both being deeply touched by the Holy Spirit. Something quite dramatic was taking place.

The following morning, both of the men gave testimony of their experience. They were strangers to each other, but they had much in common. Both had mothers who had neglected them, neither of them had known a father, they had both been brought up in children's homes, and both had tried to fill their empty father-hole in ungodly ways.

There was prayer for a new revelation of God, confessing lies believed and misjudging of God. They had forgiven parents and authority figures who represented an angry God, and renounced ungodly beliefs. This was a major part of touching their hearts and addressing some of the fears, insecurities, anger, and failures that had engulfed them.

Their longing for a father had often overwhelmed their orphan hearts. As they owned their true feelings, received forgiveness from God and forgave, the Lord revealed His heart to them. Their testimony was, "I've found the Father I've been looking for."

Each proved the faithfulness of God and the truth of His word,

> *Though my father and mother forsake me, the* LORD *will receive me.*
> (Psalm 27:10)

They were no longer orphans, but adopted children of their heavenly Father.

Every one of us who know Christ Jesus as Savior and Lord needs to have a deep knowledge in our hearts that the Father Himself loves us. Every day we need to know that we belong to the Father because we are in Jesus. Covered with the precious blood of Jesus, we belong to the Father's family. What about you? Are you constantly and joyfully aware that the Father loves you? Without this awareness a state of uncertainty, discouragement, and insecurity remains with us. We live as spiritual orphans, often independent of God instead of secure children of our Father in heaven.

Stepping Stone 11

Pray with the psalmist, "*Search me, O God, and know my heart; test me and know my anxious thoughts. See if there is any offensive way in me, and lead me in the way everlasting*" (Psalm 139:23–24).

CHAPTER

12

The Father's Embrace

I have met many believers who have received salvation, healing and deliverance, and who have been filled with the Holy Spirit, yet they do not feel secure in the Father's love. Most of them have negative thoughts about themselves, and they do not live in the true freedom of the children of God.

The Gospels repeatedly show that Jesus came to bring us to the Father. The parable of Jesus in Luke 15:11–32 that we have looked at earlier is usually known as the parable of the prodigal son, or the parable of the lost son. As I have read, reread and studied this parable, I wonder if the most appropriate title for it would be "The Parable of the Perfect Father."

The parable reveals the heart of the father. He had a son who went away and was lost, and another son who stayed at home and was still lost. The son who went away came back, and on his homecoming was embraced by his father. He had a revelation of his father's heart for him – the revelation we all need of our Father's heart for us. I would like to consider the truths Jesus was teaching about His Father and our Father as we look at the story of the Perfect Father.

The prodigal son who left home came to the end of his own resources, and decided to return to his father. He didn't know how he would be received, but he had lived in his father's house long enough to know something of his father's character. He had a true picture of his father, not an imaginary one. He returned home as he was to the father who received him back.

To meet with God, we must come to Him as we are with the knowledge that His character can be trusted, and that He will receive us. This Father is:

Patiently waiting for you to come and ready to go out and meet you

> *... while he was still a long way off, his father saw him and was filled with compassion for him ...*
>
> (v. 20)

It seems the father in the story had never stopped waiting and looking for his son to return. Did he stand on the roof of the house every day looking and longing for a sight of his returning son away in the distance?

The father ran to meet his son – he was so eager to have him home. As he runs he is filled with emotion – the emotion of compassion. He runs with open arms, not clenched fists. This father had suffered heartache as he waited for his son to return. Your heavenly Father longs for you to turn toward Him and come to Him. Tenderness and compassion fill His heart – He is not waiting in anger, but in love. He is the "God of the scars" with arms wide open to receive you. He is:

Affectionate, loving you for who you are, and not for what you do

> *... he ran to his son, threw his arms around him and kissed him.*
>
> (v. 20)

The father embraced his son. We can only imagine the thoughts of his son: "Will he be angry? What's he going to say? Will he want me back or will he send me away?" He had no need to be concerned. His father threw his arms around him, and welcomed him back home.

The father was intimate in his expression of affection. He knew how to express the overflowing emotions of his heart. He kissed his son. The expression means "kissed him repeatedly, tenderly and earnestly."

This picture of the father embracing the prodigal is critical for us to understand what God is like. Jesus is showing us a Father longing for His lost children to come home. He is longing to welcome those of us who are emotionally far away; we who have believed the lies of the evil one, and who need a revelation of His love.

Our true Father embraces us as we come to Him, falls on our necks, and weeps for joy. He created us to know Him in true relationship.

Utterly forgiving

> *The son said to [his father], "Father, I have sinned against heaven and against you. I am no longer worthy to be called your son." But the father said to his servants, "Quick! Bring the best robe and put it on him."*
>
> (vv. 21–22)

The son came home repentant. He spoke a single sentence, and that was enough. He probably still smelled of the pigsty, but his father didn't seem to notice. The son's shame would have been intense. His sin in the eyes of the neighbours would have been unforgivable, but the father's forgiveness was instant, with no strings attached.

The father placed his son under the covering and protection of a special robe. He put the best robe on his son, the robe reserved for dignitaries and important people who visited him. The robe was a sign of favor and honor. It was the father's way of saying without words, "I have forgiven my son."

Forgiveness was complete. The father didn't wait for a full explanation. Didn't say, "I'm forgiving but not forgetting." He didn't resolve to remind his son of his sin in the future if he stepped out of line. "I'm wiping the slate clean – my son is completely forgiven." The robe could be seen as a robe of righteousness – the son was restored to his father.

His forgiveness was sacrificial and restorative

The son was prepared to come home and work as a hired servant – a slave. However, his father's forgiveness could never be earned, nor could it be deserved. Forgiveness was an act of grace on his father's part. Held close by his father he received forgiveness, reconciliation, and healing from his shame.

Forgiveness is the message of the Bible, the heart of the Christian faith. It is never cheap; it is costly. It is the enduring evidence of the Father's love. Forgiveness leads to the Father's heart – it restores relationship with Him. God's nature and character is to forgive.

The Father that Jesus introduces us to longs to forgive. He does not wait to condemn. Our condemnation was borne by Jesus. No sin is too great for Him to forgive.

Unconditionally accepting

> *"Put a ring on his finger ..."*
>
> (v. 22)

The ring symbolized position in the family. It was a sign that the prodigal was accepted back into the family as a dearly loved son with all the rights and privileges involved. The words of the son to the father were, *"I am no longer worthy to be called your son."* That is how he felt as he stood in rags and tatters before his father, but the father accepted his son unconditionally as he was. God is unconditionally accepting. He doesn't put us on a self-improvement program before He accepts us. He doesn't say, "You must do better." He says, "Come as you are. I love you. Jesus has done everything needed for your acceptance as my dearly loved child."

If we are to experience the Father's embrace, we must come as the prodigal did. We must come with our sins that need to be forgiven; with our wounds that need to be healed; with our weaknesses and failures; with our past of which we may be ashamed.

Unconditionally loving

> *"Put ... sandals on his feet."*
>
> (v. 22)

Slaves didn't wear the sandals a son wore. Many slaves didn't wear sandals at all. When the shoes were put on the returning son, the father was making a clear statement – "You are not coming home to be a slave; you are coming home as my son." The relationship between master and slave bore no resemblance to that of father and son.

The father's love for his son was unconditional. What the son had done did not make the father love him less. The son was touched by the father, and received the love of his heart.

We cannot earn the Father's love. Whatever we do to honor Him will not make Him love us more. However much we displease Him and let Him down, He can never love us less. His love does not depend on something in us, and even if we cannot receive His unconditional love, nothing will make Him stop loving us.

The two most used words in the Bible to describe the love of God are "unfailing" and "enduring." Both words speak of unconditional love which is the basis of God's covenant love. He is committed to loving us. Nothing can quench God's love, and nothing we do can qualify us to receive it. Of course, to experience in reality such love we have to receive it in repentance and humility.

Many so-called mature believers find the concept of unconditional love beyond belief. In the human heart there is something of pride that says you receive because you do something. Love freely given is not human. It is divine!

The other prodigal

Rembrandt's wonderful painting *The Return of the Prodigal Son* shows him kneeling at the feet of his father with his head resting on his father's breast. Despite his wayward past, he is back home again. The painting shows the father embracing the son, safe and secure in his father's love, and sensing the beating of his fatherly heart.

In the painting, the elder son is a spectator, simply observing the scene of reconciliation. Outwardly he did everything that was right, but inwardly he never knew his father. He was cut off on the inside – bitter, resentful, jealous of his younger brother, and inwardly rebellious. On the outside he seemed the ideal son, but he was lost on the inside.

Bitterness pours from his lips to both his brother and his father. What comes from his lips comes from his heart: "For years I have slaved for you – you never even gave me a goat to celebrate with my friends." The words of his father cannot touch him: *"My son, you are always with me, and everything I have is yours"* (v. 31).

The elder brother failed to see that his father's love was not given in proportion to how well he behaved. The father never ceases to love, but a bitter heart cannot receive his love.

Like the elder brother, we too can be separated from the light of our Father's presence. We may have been "slaving" for Him for years, and still not know Him. We may even hold bitterness toward Him that will be a barrier to knowing Him. He will never stop loving you; His arms will remain open to embrace. He has never withheld His love, never stopped calling you His child, but He cannot compel. He gives each one of us the choice to come or to stay away. The choice is to come with an open heart, just as you are, to be received into His heart that is overflowing with goodness, grace, compassion, tenderness, and kindness.

Stepping Stone 12

Do you see in yourself the younger brother or the older brother, or a mixture of both? Come to God as you are, confess what is in your heart, and ask him to forgive any bitterness you have toward anyone you have judged.

CHAPTER

13

Receiving the Father's Embrace

The experience of the love of God, which is given to us by the Holy Spirit, is extraordinary. God is an intimate Father, and intimacy is a matter of the heart. True love is intimate. It cannot be expressed in words, and it is known in the heart.

Although we cannot live on an experience, we can live in a relationship. The security of living, knowing we are dearly loved and secure in the Father's love is a daily experience for those who live lives that honor the Lord Jesus.

The experience of receiving the Father's embrace is life-changing, and is for us all. There are some keys that must turn in our hearts before we can know God in reality, and love Him as He loves us. Some of these keys to receiving the Father's embrace are:

Desire to know God

The prodigal son came to his senses before he turned back to his father. Afar off he recognized what he was missing, and something in his heart awakened. Maybe it was longing, desire, desperation to be in relationship with his father.

Something in our hearts needs to be awakened – something of longing and desire for God alone. Not simply a longing for what He can do for us, but a longing for Himself like the psalmist had when he cried out,

> *As the deer pants for streams of water, so my soul pants for you, O God. My soul thirsts for God, for the living God. Where can I go and meet with God?*
>
> (Psalm 42:1–2)

Whatever desires toward Him we have are given by the Holy Spirit, so we can pray for spiritual awakening – for desire to truly know God, and become like Jesus.

Turn toward the Father

The prodigal son said, *"I will set out and go back to my father"* (v. 18). He was separated from his father, both by distance and desire, until he came to his senses. He turned around to go back to his father. In a far country, there was longing in his heart to be right, and to be reconciled to his father.

When we turn toward the Father in repentance, we are seeing things differently. To see things differently is a choice. True repentance brings with it a conscious desire to change – to be rid of the hindrances in our lives that separate us from God. Do we have that willingness to change?

Recognize how sin hurts God

The prodigal had a sense of his own unworthiness in the light of his father's unconditional love and acceptance. He felt he deserved the lowest place in his father's family. *"Father, I have sinned against heaven and against you"* (v. 21).

Sin is more than breaking God's laws; it is breaking His heart. Sin is what we do – we transgress God's laws. Another word the Bible uses for sin is iniquity – the innate sin that is within us all. The sin of what we are in the light of the holiness of God. Sin separates us from God. That is why the psalmist prayed, *"Create in me a pure heart, O God, and renew a steadfast spirit within me"* (Psalm 51:10).

Pray for a revelation of the cross

At the cross we see the extent of God's love.

> *This is how God showed his love among us: He sent his one and only Son into the world that we might live through him.*
>
> (1 John 4:9)

At the cross we also see God's hatred of the sin that separates us from Him, and what it cost Him to bring lost humankind to Himself.

At the cross we also see what love is.

> *This is how we know what love is: Jesus Christ laid down his life for us."*
>
> (1 John 3:16)

The cross is the place of sacrifice. With the cross directly before Him, Jesus asked the Father if there was another way for sinners to be redeemed (Luke 22:42). Of course, there was no other way. Jesus is the only way to the Father.

The cross is a place of outstretched arms – the cross where Jesus said, *"It is finished"* (John 19:30) is the place where we receive the Father's embrace. Jesus is the One who shows us the Father. For us to know the Father, we must know and love His Son first. Jesus reveals the inmost heart of the Father toward us, and He said, *"If you knew me, you would know my Father also"* (John 8:19).

When Jesus was preparing His disciples for His death on the cross, He assured them of the Father's love for them. They were indeed loved by His Father because they loved Jesus, and believed that He came from God (see John 16:27).

We cannot bypass the cross. When the wonder of the cross touches our hearts, we know without a doubt that we are truly loved by the Father with an amazing divine love, and it draws a response of love from our own hearts too. Pray for a revelation of the cross.

Seek the baptism of the Holy Spirit

We need to experience the Father's love to really know it, and it is the Holy Spirit who fills us with His love. We can know "*how dearly God loves us, because he has given us the Holy Spirit to fill our hearts with his love*" (Romans 5:5 NLT).

If we are to experience the Father's embrace, we need the reality of the Holy Spirit in our hearts.

> *So you have not received a spirit that makes you fearful slaves. Instead, you received God's Spirit when he adopted you as his own children. Now we call him, "Abba, Father." For his Spirit joins with our spirit to affirm that we are God's children.*
>
> (Romans 8:15–16 NLT)

As we saw in chapter 5, when we are born again we receive new spiritual life within. This new life is from God and we are taken into His family. Firstly, we are convicted of sin, and brought to repentance and faith in Jesus. Then, immediately, the Holy Spirit comes to dwell in our hearts as a seal of God's ownership. Through the indwelling Holy Spirit, God conveys to us the awareness that He is our Father and we are His children (2 Corinthians 1:21–22). Everyone who belongs to Christ is indwelt by the Holy Spirit (Romans 8:9).

In the New Testament, we read of the Holy Spirit coming upon or falling upon people (Acts 8:16; Acts 10:44). "To fall upon" can also mean "to embrace." As the father of the prodigal fell upon his son, throwing his arms around him and embracing him, so we read of the Holy Spirit falling upon believers and filling their lives with the warmth of His presence. Many people who have experienced the baptism of the Holy Spirit (Acts 1:5; Mark 1:8) have described it as a baptism of love. You are immersed in something gloriously supernatural that is outside of yourself.

The baptism in the Holy Spirit sometimes happens at the same time as a person becomes a child of God (Acts 10:44–48), and sometimes it is a subsequent experience (Acts 8:9–19), but it is a definite experience. In his book, *Leaning Into the Wind*, A.W. Tozer says that in the Bible, no believer

> ***was ever filled with the Holy Spirit who did not know he had been filled. Neither was anyone filled who did not know when he was filled. And no one was ever filled gradually.***[1]

Immediately before His ascension, Jesus told His disciples to wait in Jerusalem for the gift His Father promised which He had been talking to them about. He told them that they would be baptized with the Holy Spirit, and would be empowered for witness and service (Acts 1:4–8). After the Day of Pentecost, we see the disciples turning the world upside down, and doing the things that Jesus did. Do you recognize your need of this empowering of the Holy Spirit, so you can be effective in your life and service?

As a child of God, you cannot live your life looking back to an experience, wonderful though this may have been, but in a daily relationship of intimacy with Jesus. A normal part of this relationship is an ongoing filling with the Holy Spirit (Ephesians 5:18). He will enable you and empower you to live victoriously for Jesus in the knowledge that you are truly loved by God.

---

1. A.W. Tozer, *Leaning Into the Wind* (Milton Keynes: Authentic, 2008).

Stepping Stone 13

Pray for a new understanding of God's inexpressible love for you. If you have not been baptized in the Holy Spirit, ask for it. God has promised that if you ask, you will receive.

CHAPTER

14

Living as the Father's Child

Our Father's desire is that each of us, His children, will become increasingly like Jesus, growing more and more to live the way that Jesus lived. This process is called sanctification. It is a work of the Holy Spirit in the believer's life, and it changes us so that more of Jesus is seen in us. Sanctification is a process of getting rid of the self-life to make more room for the life of Jesus. He lived His life absolutely dependent upon His Father, listening to His voice, and uncompromisingly obeying Him (John 8:28; 12:49–50; 14:10; 14:31).

Living as the Father's child cannot rest on experience alone, wonderful though experience is. It is a life to be lived – a life of knowing Him more, and loving Him more. Each of us has been called and chosen. God's purpose is for us *"to be conformed to the likeness of His Son ..."* (Romans 8:29). We are all children in a process – the process of being made holy. We are all part of the same family – so Jesus is not ashamed to call us brothers and sisters (see Hebrews 2:11).

What does it mean to live as a child of God?

A Bible term for a child of God is someone who is "in Christ." We are in Him and He is in us. In 1 John 2:6 we read, *"Whoever claims to live in him must walk as Jesus did."* The preceding verse says that obedience is the hallmark of those who are "in him."

Living an obedient life

When the Bible talks of obedience, what it means is uncompromising obedience. It means obedience that is born out of a relationship of trust. That is the evidence that we love the One who loved us and gave Himself for us. Jesus said,

> *If anyone loves me, he will obey my teaching. My Father will love him, and we will come to him and make our home with him.*
>
> (John 14:23)

Jesus seems to be saying that if we really want His presence and the knowledge of His Father in our lives, we have no option but to obey Him. The more we know the worthiness of a person's character, the easier it is to trust and obey them. We might say then that obedience is the fruit of truly knowing God. Sometimes this kind of obedience may not be easy.

Elisabeth Elliot's husband, Jim, was murdered by the Auca Indians in Ecuador, an unreached tribe to whom he was trying to take the gospel. After a relatively short time, Elisabeth and another lady went back to the tribe that had killed her husband, taking her small daughter with them. Many people thought this unwise. Elisabeth's comment was, "Obedience is my responsibility; the consequences are God's."

Walking in the light

Light exposes things that are hidden in darkness. As children of God we no longer belong to the darkness or the night. We belong to the kingdom of light. To walk in the light means to be willing for God to expose the hidden things in our hearts. Fellowship with God is always hindered if we choose darkness over light. The effect of walking in the light is that we live in fellowship with others who are God's children, and with the Father Himself (see 1 John 1:5–7).

The light of the Lord is pure light, and in Him there is no darkness. His nature is love, but it is also light, and He is against any darkness in us. Darkness keeps us from intimacy with Him. It is good to ask Him to shine His light into any places of darkness in us, even darkness of which we are not aware.

> *The LORD's light penetrates the human spirit, exposing every hidden motive.*
>
> (Proverbs 20:27 NLT)

Jesus taught that those who belong to Him love the truth, and are willing to come into the light for scrutiny. They desire to be the same on the inside as on the outside (John 3:21).

Areas of darkness into which we need God's searchlight to shine include hidden and unconfessed sin, harboured resentment, isolation, and unreality. To walk in the light means to be real because nothing is hidden. This is an ongoing process if we are really going to walk in the light.

Walking in the truth

Walking in the truth is a pathway to freedom. Jesus said,

> *If you hold to my teaching, you are really my disciples. Then you will know the truth, and the truth will set you free.*
>
> (John 8:31–32)

To walk in the truth requires an active desire to know the truth and to obey it. Unless we know the truth as revealed in Scripture and apply it to our lives, we lose some of the freedom and reality of being a child of God; we can easily go into deception.

Walking in the truth leads to spiritual discernment so that we sense when things are not right. People who work in banks are trained to identify forged bank notes. However, during their training they are not shown forgeries; instead they handle lots of genuine notes. The more familiar you are with the real thing, the more easily you will spot a forgery. In the same way, we need to know the truth of the Word of God so that when we are faced with the counterfeit we recognize it for what it is.

This includes recognizing lies we have believed to be truth. Lies we have believed about ourselves, and lies we have believed about God that have opened doorways for fear to take a hold. Lies lead to slavery to fear.

> *It is for freedom that Christ has set us free. Stand firm, then, and do not let yourselves be burdened again by a yoke of slavery.*
>
> (Galatians 5:1)

Walking in love

To walk in love means to understand how God wants us to love. Paul said in 1 Corinthians 13 that even if we move in all the spiritual gifts, if we don't have God's kind of love, we have nothing. The Bible is not speaking of human love, but of *agape* love – God's love.

To walk in love assumes that we have received God's love for ourselves. Until we have personally experienced the love God has for us, we cannot fully love Him as He deserves to be loved, nor can we truly love our fellow humans. Only God's Spirit can enable us to love in this way (Romans 5:5), and He is the one who puts the love of God into our hearts. It doesn't come from ourselves. When we ask the Holy Spirit to give us God's love for others, He fills our cold hearts with His own love.

Walking in love will affect the choices we make. If we love God we will love His Word, read it, and let Him speak to us through it. The more we hear Him speak, the more our love for Him will grow, and from that love we will find ourselves loving those with whom we rub shoulders as we never imagined we could love them.

Loving others in the way Jesus loved them, which means allowing Jesus to love others through you, is evidence that the love of the Father is in you. Have you asked the Holy Spirit to give you this love?

Living according to the Spirit

Living according to the Spirit is the opposite of living according to the sinful nature. The sinful nature has to be put to death so that the Holy Spirit has control of our lives. Left to our own devices, the sinful nature is very strong because it is full of self. The Bible teaches that we can never heal it; we must die to it.

Living according to the Spirit is about freedom. Paul wrote,

> *... live by the Spirit, and you will not gratify the desires of the sinful nature.*
>
> (Galatians 5:16)

Living by the Spirit means to be guided and led by the Holy Spirit, the Spirit of Jesus. It means to walk as Jesus did (1 John 2:6). It involves making godly choices, right choices morally, ethically, and spiritually, making the lordship of Jesus a daily choice.

Abiding in Jesus

Abiding means restfully living in Jesus. This is the Father's way for His children to live fruitful lives. He will prune and cleanse the areas of our lives that are less fruitful. Fruitfulness in our lives brings glory to our Father. Jesus said, *"This is to my Father's glory, that you bear much fruit, showing yourselves to be my disciples"* (John 15:8).

Abiding in Jesus implies that we commit ourselves to Him. Having been forgiven and cleansed by His blood, we have received His grace, and now we choose to merge our will with His. To abide in Jesus means we are committed to doing His will. It means that we are one with Him, and that we live in a place of rest.

The more closely we abide in Jesus, the more secure we are in His love and the Father's love. As we abide, the Holy Spirit continually fills our lives with the love of Jesus, and fills us with inexpressible joy.

Living in the fear of the Lord

The fear of the Lord can be described as reverential trust. As His children, He expects us to trust Him because we know Him, and also to reverence Him for the powerful God He is. His nature and His character will always be the same.

I was recently involved in a Bible study on the fear of the Lord with some young people. They found the concept of fearing the Lord difficult to comprehend until one of them stumbled upon a Bible verse:

> *... the fear of God will ... keep you from sinning.*
>
> (Exodus 20:20)

When read in its context, the whole concept of the fear of the Lord made sense.

This amazing God who is our Father is also King of kings and Lord of lords, creator and ruler of the universe. He can be, and

He desires to be, intimately known by us, but He is altogether different to us and we should reverence Him.

Conclusion

To live your life day by day as the Father's child is to live a life of wonder at His amazing love and grace, and to live a life of peace and security, knowing He is altogether trustworthy. We each have a past and a future. Every child is precious, and will never be out of His sight or out of His mind. He knows us as no other ever could, and He will never forget us. He loves and cares for each individual child as if there were no other. You are never out of His mind; your name is engraved on the palms of His hands (see Isaiah 49:16).

He will deal with your past as you trust His wisdom; He holds your future in His hands, and in that knowledge you can find hope in the present. He is the great "I am," the God of the present, who will never leave you nor forsake you.

I conclude this book with a reflection on the faithfulness of God in the past which inspires faith for the future as a final stepping stone to the Father's heart.

Dear Father,
In the past You have been my shelter and refuge, whether in joy or despair.

You have spoken into my life when I most needed it.

You have been faithful to all your promises, whether I have been strong or fearful.

You have calmed me in suffering, and shone Your light into the darkest recesses of my heart.

Lord, I trust You today.

Appendix

About Ellel Ministries

www.ellel.org

Our Vision

Ellel Ministries is a non-denominational Christian Mission Organization with a vision to resource and equip the Church by welcoming people, teaching them about the Kingdom of God and healing those in need (Luke 9:11).

Our Mission

Our mission is to fulfill the above vision throughout the world, as God opens the doors, in accordance with the Great Commission of Jesus and the calling of the Church to proclaim the Kingdom of God by preaching the good news, healing the broken-hearted and setting the captives free. We are, therefore, committed to evangelism, healing, deliverance, discipleship and training. The particular scriptures on which our mission is founded are Isaiah 61:1–7; Matthew 28:18–20; Luke 9:1–2; 9:11; Ephesians 4:12; 2 Timothy 2:2.

Our Basis of Faith

God is a Trinity. God the Father loves all people. God the Son, Jesus Christ, is Savior and Healer, Lord and King. God the Holy Spirit indwells Christians and imparts the dynamic power by which they are enabled to continue Christ's ministry. The Bible is the divinely inspired authority in matters of faith, doctrine and conduct, and is the basis for teaching.

Ellel Ministries International
Ellel Grange,
Ellel,
Lancaster, LA2 0HN
United Kingdom

Sovereign World Ltd

For details of new titles
and information about all Sovereign World's books,
please go to:
www.sovereignworld.com

or write to the company at the headquarters address:

Sovereign World Ltd.,

P.O.Box 784,
Ellel,
Lancaster,
LA1 9DA
United Kingdom

Or send us an email to:
info@sovereignworld.com

Most books are also available in e-book format and can be purchased online.